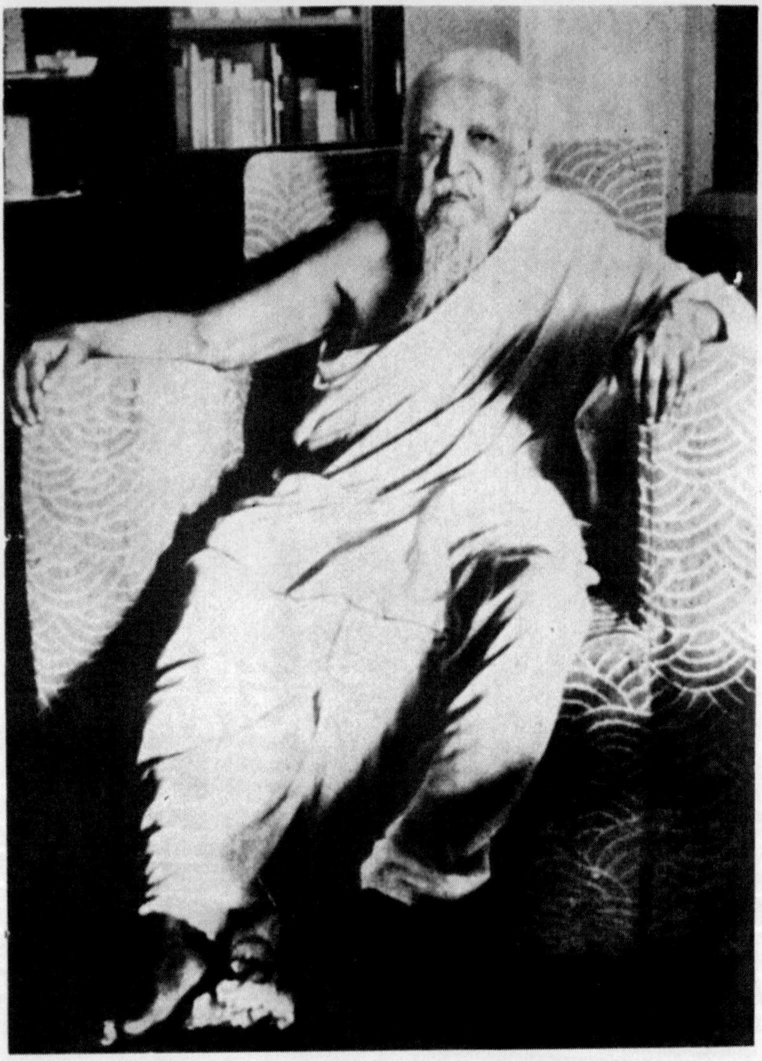

Savitri Series

SAVITRI UNVEILED

A Selection

SYED MEHDI IMAM
M. A. (Oxon.) Bar-at-Law

VERITAS VINCIT OMNIA
Truth Conquereth all things

MOTILAL BANARSIDASS
Delhi :: Varanasi :: Patna

Indological Publishers & Booksellers
Head Office : Bungalow Road, Jawahar Nagar, Delhi-7
Branches : 1. Chowk, Varanasi-1 (U.P.)
2. Ashok Rajpath, Patna-4 (Bihar)

First Edition: Delhi, 1980

Printed in India
By Shantilal Jain, at Shri Jainendra Press, A-45, Phase-I,
Industrial Area, Naraina, New Delhi-110 028.
Published by Narendra Prakash Jain, for Motilal Banarsidass,
Bungalow Road, Jawahar Nagar, Delhi-110 007.

सत्यमेव जयते

प्रधान मन्त्री भारत

PRIME MINISTER
INDIA

FOREWORD

Syed Mehdi Imam renounced a distinguished career in law to devote himself to his philosophical pursuits. His "Drama of Prince Arjuna" showed deep understanding of the Bhagavad Gita and of the spiritual heritage of India.

The present work is an interpretation of the thought of one of the great sages our country has produced - Sri Aurobindo. I hope that it will find resonance in the hearts of other seekers of truth.

(Indira Gandhi)

New Delhi,
March 23, 1980

Blessings

DEDICATION TO THE MOTHER
THE MESSENGER

"So it was when Jesus came in his gentleness with his Divine Compassion and great Gospel of Peace, men hail'd him and in the title of Christ Crown'd him with love beyond all earth-names of renown. For He, wandering unarmed saved by the Spirit's flame, in few years, with few friends founded a world-empire wider than Alexander's and more enduring."

Testament of Beauty : Robert Bridges.

FRANCE

O France, where are thy glories gone ? Austerlitz, Jena and Marengo are no more. Napoleon sleeps under the dome of the Invalides, Fallen are the walls of the Bastile; Vanished the palaces of the Tuileries. Twice in this century have thine arches, columns and colonnades heard the tramp of armed heels. Yet Vichy's polluted breath has not stained thy scutcheon or thy sword. O risen France, thou knowest not thy fortune or thy fate. The voice of Domremy[1] is heard once again in thy clandestine air . O City of Paris,[2] Mother of Arts, on a windless morn didst thou bring to birth in a cradle rare the first Madonna of the Supramental Light. Her did the predestined breezes bear across the azurous seas to Hindustan's holy sands. By Pondicherry's palm-fringed shore, assaulting the roar of the everlasting main, springs the first fane[3] of the Supramental Ray. From Europe's frost, from Montreal's freezing lakes; from Florida's warming gulfs and Missisippi's rolling flood; from Nile's sinuous streams and Zion's hallowed hill: from Nairobi's sunlit lands; from the vast

1. Domremy: The village where Joan of Arc heard the heavenly voices.

2. The Mother was born in Paris on the 21st of February 1878.

3. First fane: The Aurobindo Ashram in Pondicherry with its affiliations throughout the globe.

wash of the Australasian seas where the masts and antennae of new Canberra gleam; from the waters of the Eastern foam where Tokyo's terraces and Yokihama's glittering crest hail the surf; from Peking's ancient walls and Hongkong's crowded quay; from Russia's chilly steppes by the fringe of the Arctic lights where the aureate domes of the Kremlin glow; there by the Master's shrine, robed in wreaths of flowers and coruscate with light, the people of the earth gather to salute the Messenger and the Message. Hard by Pondicherry's widening bay where the soft surf in an inland murmur sings, under a canopy of rarest blue rises UNESCO's dream the far facades of famed Auroville[4] the first City of the Nations, the symbol of human harmony and universal delight.

O Mother of the Supramental Light, O Madonna of my dreams, from this hand and heart dedicated take these few frail flowers of my thought plucked from the garden of aspiration. These rosebuds odorous and lily blooms dank with dew, violets shy and bluebells tremulous, myrtle-leaf and bay-leaf verdurous and, the queen of the orchard, the seven-petalled lotus of the seven ecstasies, cherish with the rain-drops of thy love. From the still city of the white beatitudes where all the charms of all the Muses dwell, breathe upon my brows the suspirations of the power to render into rhymeless rhyme the rich radiances of the reveries of Savitri.

Sri Aurobindo Ashram
Pondicherry, 21. 2. 71

S. M. I.

4. Auroville; The City of the Nations built under the auspices of UNESCO about eight miles from Pondicherry in fulfilment of Sri Aurobindo's Ideal of human unity.

PREFACE

What is 'Savitri'

Savitri means light. Savitri is the Epic poem of Sri Aurobindo. It is his major work. Savitri is the light of God. The poem deals with the light of God which transforms the mind of man into the light of God.

The Present Selection

The present Selection is a Selection from Savitri. It is connected with head lines and sub-head lines and accompanied by commentary and notes which are essential for the proper appreciation of the Epic. The subject covers the whole of Savitri in brief selection. The whole of Savitri moves into a single pattern. Savitri is unified. The poem is integrated. The Selections read as a continuous movement of the Epic.

The Nature of the Selection

The present selection is intended for Colleges and universities and students for the higher class in English. Savitri is set in the University syllabus but without unification and support of a commentary head lines or notes. In my opinion the selection is fit to be prescribed in university syllabuses in India.

I would also recommend the book to Educational authorities in India and particularly to the authorities of UNESCO where this selection may be a part of the UNESCO library of the great literature of India, now in English comparable to ancient literatures of the Vedas and Upanishads.

Neora House,
Bank Road, Patna-1
5th April 1980.

(Syed Wasiudeen)
Sometime a Judge of
the High Court, Patna and
Jammu & Kashmir
High Court.

CONTENTS

Introduction

THE SUPRAMENTAL TRANSFORMATION

And I saw a new heaven and a new earth; for the first heaven and the first earth were passed away.
Rev. Ch. 21, V. 1

The Scope of the Selections

Of the thirty volumes of the Collected works of Sri Aurobindo which now stand on the book-shelf of world readers, the greatest and most perfect in style and finish, in depth and range is *Savitri*. This great work consisting of nearly twentyfour thousand lines runs into eight hundred pages of print. The massive proportions of this masterpiece of literature demands condensation. We have therefore reduced *Savitri* into eightyfour critical passages supplemented by commentary, notes and appendices. Our purpose is to present the point and substance of the poem in the briefest compass.

For the clarity of understanding each selection is connected with a headline and sub-headline. Thereafter follows the text. Below the text is a commentary which echoes the sense of *Savitri* in language of rhythmic prose akin to poetry. Then in close sequence come the detailed notes of extreme conciseness which seek in flashes to reveal the subterranean depths of the verses of *Savitri*.

These selections are intended to prepare the first readers of *Savitri* with the knowledge of the main movements of the poem. When the audience of the future have been awakened to the wonders of the Epic which challenges the grandeur of *Paradise Lost* and the *Divine Comedy* the perusing public will not fail to press forward to the reading of the complete *Savitri*.

The Integral Yoga

The base of the integral Yoga which lies in the background of *Savitri* is not a transcendence out of Matter and Mind into the Light of God. The yoga of Sri Aurobindo envisages a transformation of Mind, Matter and Life into Supermind. It distinguishes between a flight into the abode of God, and a permanent transformation of the earth—life into Light. For the better understanding of the point, we may use an image. When a caterpillar goes into sleep in its chrysalis of matter and then finds a new awakening as the body of a butterfly in the environment of the new air, this is the transformation of the form of the caterpillar. It is not an escape but a transmutation. In the realisation of the Yoga Sri Aurobindo saw that the main constituents of our being, our Body, our Mind, our Life were asleep in a world of nescience. He also discovered in the depths of our being that the Light of God was secretly concealed in Matter, Mind and Life. That Light Sri Aurobindo called the Light of Supermind. Sri Aurobindo also watched the emergence of the Supramental Light from Matter, Mind and Life into the Light of God under the descent of the Supramental Force. In the long preparations of his Yoga he noted the ascents of Mind transcendencies into Supermind. He realised that these ascensions from Mind into Supermind did not truly transmute the field of Matter. Then he perceived that in the scheme of the ascensions there was implicit a descent of the Force. This he called the Force of the Supramental Light. Thus his yoga took a double turn. It took the way of the ascent and the way of the descent of the force. From his repeated ascensions from Mind to Supermind, and from the repeated descents of the Supermind into Mind, Sri Aurobindo marked the gradual transformation of his body into Supermind. In our imagery the caterpillar was turned into the butterfly in a new body and in a new range of being. In a word, he experienced the complete transmutation of Body and Mind into the Supramental Light.

In the gradual growth of his yoga, in the supramental consciousness, he moved into the fields of the subtle substances which he called the fields of ascending Matter. The lowest field of Matter he called the field of the Mind of Night. The entanglement of the soul in the lower substance he called the Knot of Matter. From the Mind of Night he rose into the next grade of substance which he called the world of the Intuitive Mind. Then he ascended into the next grade of substance the Mind of Light.

Thence he found an Intermediate World of being—the Overmind. The world of the Overmind was a link between the Mind of Light, the Intuitive Mind and the Mind of Night below and the Supermind the region of the Creative Ray. Thence he passed beyond the fields of the Supermind into the Triune Ecstasies of the Light. Also, he formulated his experience of the descent from the Absolute Light back to the realms of Supermind, Overmind and thence into the Mind of Light, the Intuitive Mind and the Mind of Night.

The Life Divine and the Epic of Savitri

The above formulation of the ascent from Mind of Night to the Absolute and the descent of the Absolute down the ladder of being into Matter is fully described in *Savitri.* The upward movement from the Mind of Night to the Absolute and the downward movement from the Absolute into the Mind of Night are presented for clearer understanding in the chart below.

THE SCHEME OF THE ASCENT FROM MIND TO THE ABSOLUTE AND THE DESENT FROM THE ABSOLUTE TO THE MIND OF NIGHT

ASCENT		
A		THE TRIUNE ECSTASIES OR THE ABSOLUTE (The Field of the Uncreated Ray)
	THE UPPER TRILOGY	SUPERMIND (Creator of all the Fields of Matter)
		OVERMIND (The Link between Supermind, Mind, Mind of Light and Intuitive Mind)
	THE LOWER TRILOGY	MIND OF LIGHT THE INTUITIVE MIND MIND OF NIGHT OR KNOT OF MATTER
DESCENT		

MIND | MATTER | LIFE | PSYCHE OR SOUL

The Upper Trilogy

The Upper Trilogy is the hemisphere of the Triune Ecstasies, Supermind and Overmind.

The Triune Ecstasies

This is the field of the Uncreated Ray, the Absolute. It shines upon the summit of the ascent and also at the base of the descent. For it is the All. Nowhere is it absent. It is not the Creator nor is it the Created. It is the Lord of Creation and is therefore free of creation. It is the Unmanifest which manifests Light. It is the Triune Principle of Conscious Existence, Conscious Force and Conscious Bliss. Its three Ecstasies form the supreme play or lila of Existence, Force and Bliss.

Supermind

Supermind is the Absolute Power of the Uncreated Ray which creates all the fields of Matter from the formless fields of the Uncreated Ray down into the Mind of Night. It is the first veil of the Absolute Light and is therefore Light. It is the first emanation of the Absolute Existence and is therefore the pure Existence. It is the first Manifestation of the Absolute Bliss and is therefore the Bliss. It is the first expression of the Triune Ecstasies and is therefore the seal of all the Ecstasies. As it is Creator of the Overmind, the Mind of Light, the Intuitive Mind, and the Mind of Night, it is secretly contained in all substances of our being, material of immaterial.

Overmind

In this first experience of the higher ranges of the Light, Sri Aurobindo tells us that when he reached the Light of the Overmind he mistook it for the Light of the Supermind. His subsequent realisations of the Integral Yoga showed him that the Overmental experience was only the prelude of higher realisations of the world of the Supermind. The Overmind is therefore an intermediate world of Light embracing the higher substances of the Upper Trilogy and the grosser matter of the Lower Trilogy. The Overmind is as it were a buffer kingdom between the aureate Rays of the Supermind and the darkened terrain of Matter.

The Lower Trilogy

The Lower Trilogy is formed of the Mind of Light, the Mind of the Intuitions, and the Mind of Night with the corollaries of the Knot of Matter which are termed Mind, Matter, Life and the Psyche.

Mind of Light

The dazzling beams of the Supermind, tempered by the veiling Rays of the Overmind on their first descent fall into the kingdom of the Mind of Light. In it the gross substance of the Mind of Night grows tenuous and subtle. The smoke of the dark abyss of Matter does not touch it. Matter is attenuated into Light. The sluggard atoms of Matter become the supersensuous substance of the Mind of Light.

Intuitive Mind

In the Intuitive Mind, the Mind of Light grows dim. The Intuitive Mind springs from the well-heads of Matter. But, because the Mind of Light is secretly inherent as a percept in the folds of the Intuitive Mind, the Mind of intuitions is filled with the flashes of the superior realms of the Light.

Mind of Night

The Mind of Night, in the last crypt of substance, envelopes the worlds of Matter with the shadows of nescience. It is the field of phenomena so dark, so dismal, so deep, that hand cannot see hand. In its black domains the light of the Absolute no more seems to shine. It is the final descent of the Light of God into the darkened abysm of Inconscience.

Knot of Matter

The Knot of Matter is the last corrosion of the Light. Born of the womb of the Mind of Night, it is the servitor of the Night. Mind is the last obscurer of the kingdom of the Triune

Ecstasies. Its fellow creature and colleague, Matter is the delver of the deepest densities of the realms of nescience. In a secret pact with the Mind of Night, Life plays a vast drama in the theatre of darkness. Behind Matter and Mind is the silent spectator the Psyche which waits in sealed depths for the arrival of the secret footfalls of the Supermind which shall free mortality from the bonds of the Mind of Night.

The Involution of the Ray

In its descent from the Absolute into the wells of nescient Matter, the Radiance of the Triune Ecstasies dims and frames the first Mask of the Supreme Light. In the Supermind is the first concealment of the Supernature. In the fall into the fields of the Overmind is the second mask of the Absolute. In the Fields of the Upper Trilogy of the Triune Ecstasies, Supermind and Overmind, the veils that cover the Infinite are the rarest. As these are domains of the Light there is no darkening of Matter. In the descent from the Supermind and Overmind into the Mind of Light is the third veil of the Divine Spirit. As the Mind of Light is the plane of Light the shade of densities is the subtlest. In the world of the Intuition is the fourth veil of the Spirit. Its substance is darker and its light is dimmer as the fumes of the abyss of Matter ascend to mingle Light with Darkness. The Mind of Night is the last ravine of the Light. In the fathomless abyss of Matter, Mind and Life are the fifth veil of the Light.

In the five falls and the five veils of the Divine behind the mask stands the Absolute in total concealment.

The Evolution of the Ray

Because the Absolute Spirit is involved in the Triune Ecstasies and in the descending planes of Supermind, Overmind, Mind of Light, Mind of Intuitions and the Mind of Night it must emerge from the darkness into Light. In the evolution from the Mind of Night into the Absolute there is the great unveiling of which Savitri is the symbol. In the ascent from the Mind of Night into the Mind of Intuition is the first lifting of the veil of nescient Matter. There the rare substance of the Intuitions is freed from the densities of Matter. In the upward progress from the Mind of the Intuitions into the Mind of Light is a second unmasking of the Triune Ecstasies. There tenuous Matter is the substitute for the substance of the gross domains. In the climb from the Mind of Light into the Overmind is the third revealing. There Substance, gross or rate, is one with the forms of the Overmental Light. In the ascension from the Overmind into the Supermind is the fourth abandonment of the screens of the Absolute.

There Substance is Light and Light is Substance; the Formless is the Form and the Form is the Formless. In the fifth ascension into the fields of the Triune Ecstasies there are no masks of Matter, no veils of Light. There is a last unfolding. There is the final attaining. There the Spirit of the five ascensions merges into union with the Oversoul of the Unmanifest.

In the veiling and the unveiling of the Absolute Ray is thus the stupendous theatre of the struggles of *Savitri.*

The Play of the Superconscious Force of the Absolute

The descent and the ascent of the Spirit is the play of the Conscious Force of the Absolute. In the fall from the Infinite Spirit into the Knot of Matter, the Absolute in a dynamic drive creates the densities of Matter. In a counter-action, the ascending Force of the Absolute pushes the soul of nescience back in ascensions into the plane of the Bliss. In the ascensions of the human spirit the Conscious Force of the Absolute arranges the impediments of the Asuric Force — the subtle resistance of Matter, Mind and Life — to stabilise the flight into the fields of the Triune Ecstasies.

The Transformation of Matter into Supermind

As the secret Supermind is subtly hidden in Matter the latent Light breaks all the veils of substance. As Matter is Light, Light it becomes. As in the devolution of the Ray is implicit the evolution of the Light, so in the deep densities of Matter is implicit the manifestation of the Light.

The Drama of the Ray

Savitri is the drama of the Ray. She is the symbol of the Light of the Supermind. Because her work is in Matter's blind domain to the prayer of Aswapathy she falls as the embodied

Ray into the earth sphere. But behind the veil of her body is the Power of the Supramental Light. In the world of Appearance Savitri plays the part of the Appearances. Matter attracts Matter. Savitri attracts Satyavan. In the greenwood of a forest she meets the eyes of Satyavan. The earthly love seeks the bridegroom of earth. Savitri consents to play in the field of the veils as a veil. In the playground of nescience she meets the lord of nescience Yama. The Asuric Force exercises over Savitri the first sovereignty of the dark. Yama by a subtle stroke of Asuring malevolence withdraws Satyavan from the arms of Savitri. In Death's unholy hold the veiled Savitri asserts the Absolute potencies of the Uncreated Ray. Through the cosmic Power she unveils the mask of Yama. Death she destroys by Light. Behind the mask of Yama, Savitri's supreme revealing finds the face of the perfect, the Alone, the one. The discovered Absolute renders back to Savitri the body of Satyavan. But Savitri the creature of earth, seeks no repose with Satyavan in the field of the higher ascensions. In a swift descent from the fields of the Ray she returns with Satyavan to her task, the transmutation of Earth into Supramental Light.

Characters of the Epic

Aswapathy : Aswapathy is the symbol of the Yoga of Ascent. From the Mind of Night, from all the Knots of Matter, Mind and Life, the Spirit of Aswapathy seeking the Absolute Ray, ascends in growing strength into the Mind of the Intuitions. Dissatisfied his aspiration lifts him into the Mind of Light. Thence, in a revelry of delight, he beholds the shimmering ranges of the Overmind. In a yet more daring flight his Spirit explores the subtle skies of the Supermind. Lifted higher by the hurricane of the Force, he lies prone in a vast surrender before the throne of the Triune Ecstasies. Thence his aspiring soul returns down the Ladder of Being into the planes of Supermind, Overmind, Mind of Light and the Mind of Intuition. There swooning in the ecstasies he drifts under the driving gales of the Force into the Mind of Night and the Knot of Matter. After the ascents and descents he seeks the wider fulfilment of the transformation into the Supermind. In the Yoga of his ascents and descents he secures a constant lodging in the

Light of Supermind. The fervour of his aspiration calls a power to transform his material being into Light. In answer to his prayer the Absolute transmits a Ray. Savitri the embodied light sets the flame to his whole being. The descending Force of the Supramental Light transmutes Aswapathy into Light.

Savitri : Savitri is the symbol of the Yoga of Descent. Although she is the Light of the Supermind, the sphere of her work is the earth. As the earth is not darkness but Light, it is the Light she seeks to bring out of the depths of Matter. Savitri is the Ray veiled. She is the screen and mask of Body, Mind and Life. In Savitri is the concealment of the Light. But, because she is the Light itself she challenges the Power of the dark. Her struggle with Yama is the symbol of the struggle of the Light to break out of the shell of Matter. Savitri is the figure of the Light unveiling the webs of Matter.

Aswapathy and Savitri have not only the kinship of the flesh. They have the fellowship of the Light. The Yoga of the Ascent of Aswapathy is not a separate movement. The Yoga of the Ascent to Spirit is linked with the Yoga of Descent of the Light into Matter. In the ascending and the descending Force of Aswapathy and Savitri is a conjunction which forms the basic experience of the Integral Yoga.

Yama : Yama, the God of Death, is a symbol of the obstruction of Matter to the flight of the Spirit into the realms of Light. Yama is the mask of the Uncreated Ray. His unveiling is wrought by the veiled hand of Savitri.

In the characters of Aswapathy, Yama and Savitri is found the full circle of the Supramental evolution. In them are shown the masking and unmasking of the Absolute.

Satyavan : Satyavan is in the precarious poise of all the Yogas. He is the symbol of the incertitude of Matter. True yoga necessitates a mastery over the forces of the Dark. In the dim Satyavan seeks the power of the Light. The Light, knowing the Dark, comes to Satyavan in the form of Savitri.

Minor Characters of the Epic

The Queen gracious, but alarmed for the safety of Satyavan and Savitri, and Narad, the chief counsellor in the court of

Aswapathy, are the detached spectators of the drama of Aswapathy, Savitri and the God of death Yama.

The Legend of Savitri

The Legend of *Savitri* is drawn from the Epic of the Mahabharata. Briefly the story runs thus. In the days of old when all kings were Rishis, Aswapathy sovereign of the throne of Madra being without child sought in his austerities the birth of child of God in Matter. In occult answer to his prayer was born to his Queen a daughter. The parents named her *Savitri.* When the girl came to womanhood, no hand dared touch her hand. The aweful light within her shook the eyes of lovers. So her father told her to go forth in her own way and in her own chariot into the forest of his kingdom in quest of one who would love and cherish her. In two years she returned to her father's palace. There she told her parents that the choice of her eye fell upon Satyavan son of Dyumatsen, the eyeless king of Shalwa exiled from his native land by the work of scheming men. But in the court at the time was present another man of wisdom. His name was Narad. Narad looked into the eyes of Savitri and in the starry glance knew her fortune and her fate. He whispered into the ears of Aswapathy and the Queen that, Satyavan would leave the body's spell in a brief twelve months. But Savitri trembled not in her radiant body. She pledged her heart without fear to Satyavan and Satyavan gave his lips to Savitri. The lovers were wedded under solemn rites and lived together for twelve months. But Yama the God of Death looked askance at their wedding. At an appointed hour and date, fixed by destiny whilst Satyavan was cutting the forest wood for fire, Yama threw the noose of death about the brows of Satyavan. But Savitri the daughter of the Supramental Light flew to the court of Yama, and disputed with the God of Death for the soul of Satyavan. In all the rounds of subtle matter she pursued the heels of Yama. At last Savitri broke the lance and shield of the God of Death. For Savitri herself was the Light occult. Before her ray Yama dropped the Mask of Death. Yama tempted Savitri and bade her leave the fields of suffering earth for the palms of Paradise. But Savitri saw the trick of Yama. She demanded of God the arms of Satyavan for work on earth.

And God consented. Thus Satyavan was restored to the lips of Savitri. And Savitri and Satyavan returned hand in hand to transmute earth into Light.

The Symbol of Savitri

Savitri is the symbol of the Light of God. Because the eyes of nescience cannot bear the beams of God, God shrouds himself in the veils of Matter. Savitri is also the symbol of the veiling of the Light of God. But because God loves the sons of darkness and wants them to become the children of the Light, He throws off the mask of tears. Savitri is also a symbol of the unveiling of the Light of God.

The Composition of Savitri

Sri Aurobindo began the composition of *Savitri* in 1910 and finished the last line and the last verse in 1950 just before his liberation in Pondicherry on the 5th December, 1950. During the forty years of the composition, Savitri was cast and re-cast into fresh moulds. The great epic was the seal of Sri Aurobindo's greatest work in letters. It kept pace with the growth of his experiences of his Yoga. It was only when the realisation was complete that the Epic was closed.

The Literary Aspects of Savitri

In scope and range *Savitri* challenges the measure of the "Iliad" and the "Odyssey", the "Aeneid", and Milton's "Paradise Lost". The full story of Savitri is told in Vanaparva of the Mahabharata (Cantos 291-97) The present summary of the Legend is given in the light of the Epic of Sri Aurobindo and not in the light of the Mahabharata. The metre of *Savitri* in the Miltonic tradition has the best of the iambic with subtle variations. In his letters on *Savitri*, Sri Aurobindo wrote thus: "Savitri, is blank verse without enjambment (except rarely) each line a thing by itself and arranged in paragraphs of one, two three, four, five lines (rarely longer series), in an attempt to catch something of the Upanishadic and Kalidasian movement, so far as is possible in English."

In respect of Substance *Savitri* seeks a new range of the Epic. Whilst the "Iliad" of Homer deals with the War of Troy;

the "Odyssey" with the Wanderings of Ulysses; the "Aeneid" with the rise of Imperial Rome; and "Paradise Lost" with the expulsion of Adam and Eve from Eden's murmuring brooks, *Savitri* breaks with all previous traditions of epic poetry. Its subject is the transformation of Earth into Supermind. In respect of Epic Poetry, the nearest approach to Savitri is the "Divine Comedy" of Dante wherein the poet, at first led by Virgil, Human Reason, and later by Beatrice, the symbol of the Light, rises from the darkness of Hell and passes through cleansing fires of Purgatory to emerge into the plane of Paradise. Here the comparison ends. Dante experiences no transformation of Body, Mind and Life. His trance like the swoon of Aswapathy is an ascension into Light. It is temporary transcendence of Matter. There is no descent of the Light for transmutation. Beatrice is not Savitri. Savitri speaks with certitude of the Truth which is in the heart of every being. The poem begins with the Truth and ends with the Truth. For Truth is the substance of Sri Aurobindo's Song.

The Divisions of the Epic

Savitri is divided in accordance with the Epic tradition into Twelve Books. Books I-III unfold the Yoga of the Ascent of Aswapathy from Matter into Supermind. Books IV-VII relate to the quest of Savitri for her bridegroom Satyavan. Books VIII-XII are concerned with the Yoga of Descent of Savitri with her conquest of the shade of Death and with her transfiguration of the earth-life into Supermind.

The Conclusion

Close the window. Draw the curtains. Open the pages of *Savitri*. What do you hope to find ? Light ? No; In the kingdom of the shadows there lurks the King of shadows—Death. Read and learn. What would you read ? What would you learn ? Know then that the God of Death is the God of Light. Yama is Savitri.

SELECTIONS

THE UNIVERSAL PRAYER

In the name of God the Clement
The True, the Vast; aid and help
O Lumen Christi of Olivet;
Bright Jehovah's beam from Zion's hill;
Ray serene of Hira's holy cave;
O Nirvanic Light from forests dim of subtlest ooze and drip
O Lamp of Osiris from Nile's bank of rarest glow and gleam;
O fire in the bush on Sinai's leafy wood;
O mysteries of Eleusis in Hellas's dappled dales;
Illumine, guard and guide our reading of Savitri.

PEACE PEACE PEACE

AUM

1

NIGHT

The Night of Ignorance precedes the
Dawn of the Supramental Manifestation.

It was the hour before the Gods awake.
Across the path of the divine Event
The huge foreboding mind of Night, alone
In her unlit temple of eternity.
Lay stretched immobile upon Silence's marge.
Almost one felt, opaque, impenetrable,
In the sombre symbol of her eyeless muse
The abysm of the unbodied Infinite;

A fathomless Zero occupied the world
A power of fallen boundless self awake
Between the first and the last Nothingness
Recalling the tenebrous womb from which it came,
Turned from the insoluble mystery of birth
And the tardy process of mortality
And longed to reach its end in vacant Nought.
As in a dark beginning of all things
A mute featureless semblance of the Unknown
Repeating for ever the unconscious act,
Prolonging for ever the unseeing will
Cradled the cosmic drowse of ignorant Force
Whose moved creative slumber kindles the suns
And carries our lives in its somnambulist whirl.
Athwart the vain enormous trance of Space,
Its formless stupor without mind or life
A shadow spinning through a soulless Void
Thrown back once more into unthinking dreams,
Earth wheeled abandoned in the hollow gulfs,
Forgetful of her spirit and her fate.

Savitri: Book I: canto 1, pp 3-4

COMMENTARY

And the light shineth in darkness and the darkness comprehended it not *St. John* Chap I. Verse 5

THE REIGN OF THE ASURIC NIGHT

In the beginning was the dark and the dark knew not the Light. For the dark was contending with the Light for the dominions of the day. In the dim studios of Death, where no ray is, the Asuras devised a design to blot out Light and to establish the kingdom of the Night in the Kingdom of the Day. Because they had no light they formed a shadow; and that shadow they called the Mind of Night. And because the shadow could not see, the Mind of Night created a kingdom of shadows. It enveloped all the realm of nescience. It put the seal of sleep upon all that lives and so all things slumbered as if God was not. And the demons of Death shrouded the temple of Light in the smoke of hell. And the shrine of the Everlasting became the shrine of the Asura.

But in the body of the dark was screened in many veils the subtle Light moving towards a Divine Event, the transmutation of the Matter into the Face of the Light. But the Sons of Darkness refused to listen to the voice of the Light. Therefore the bodiless Ray vanished from the abysm of substance. In the place of Light was a zero of the worlds. For when the Light was not, nothing was. But nothingness concealed the Light. Nescience craved for the birth of the Light in the dumb vacancies of matter and the Light heard its cry. Creeping, unknown secret it urged the cosmic drowse of Matter to return to the Rays of the Day. But Matter and Mind resisted the pressure of the Light. And the Light withdrew and the Night of the Asuras began. In the vast trance of space in a formless stupor the earth whirled in the hollow gulfs of matter oblivious of the Light. For the hour was the hour of the Asuras.

Yet there was a secret word— a jewelled word—in the ear of the Night. The dark was in truth not the rival of the Light nor was Light the rival of the dark. Both the darkness and the Light were thc phases of the Supramental manifestation. The hour of the Asuras was also the hour of God. The Symbol of Night was also the symbol of the Supramental Dawn shattering the craven Power of the Dark. In obedience to the fiat of the Supreme, the dominions of the Night were to become the dominions of the Day.

DETAILED NOTES

1. *The Hour*

   The hour of the Asuric Night.

2. *Gods*

   The seers of the Light asleep in nescience.

3. *The Divine Event*

   The ultimate mystery of the transmutation of Matter, Mind and Life into Light.

4. *Mind of Night*

   The Mind of the Asuras.

5. *Alone*

   The sole sovereignty of the Mind of the Asuras.

6. *Temple of Eternity*

   The shrine of the Most High wrapped in the fumes of Hell.

7. *Immobile*

   The Cosmic Force of the dark.

8. *Upon Silence's Marge*

   The hidden worlds of Matter whirling in silence by the margin of the physical kingdom.

9. *Eyeless Muse*

   The blind figure of Matter asleep in nescience.

10. *Abysm*

    The abysm of Matter in which the unembodied Light dwells

11. *Zero*

    The Nihil of Matter when Light is extinguished by the Asuric Night.

12. *Boundless Self*

    The boundless Infinite in apparent fall into finitude.

13. *The First and the Last Nothingness*

    To the eyes of nescience everything is a Void. But to the supernal wisdom the Void is the Full because God is in the womb of the Void. Both the first Nothingness, the invisible plane of the Uncreated Ray, and the last Nothingness in the invisible planes of subtle Matter, are unbeholden of the eyes of ignorance.

14. *Mystery of Birth*

The emergence of Supermind from the secret folds of Matter, Mind and Life.

.5. *Tardy Process*

The evolution from Mind to Supermind.

16. *Vacant Nought*

The unseen Light in the heart of Nescience.

17. *Unknown*

The secret force of Supermind.

18. *Ignorant Force*

The force of the Asuras in the kingdom of nescience.

19. *Trance of Space*

The trance of the Matter in the Sphere of Nescience.

20. *Formless Stupor*

The trance of the Asuric Night.

21. *Earth forgetful of her spirit*

The earth oblivious of her ultimate change into Light.

22. *Hollow Gulfs*

The Void of Matter.

2

BIRTH

The Light of the Supramental Sun
visible on the horizon abolishes Night.

A long lone line of hesitating hue
Like a vague smile tempting a desert heart
Troubled the far rim of Life's obscure sleep.
Arrived from the other side of boundlessness
An eye of deity pierced through the dumb deeps;
A scout in a reconnaissance from the sun,

It seemed amid a heavy cosmic rest,
The torpor of a sick and weary world,
To seek for a spirit sole and desolate
Too fallen to recollect forgotten bliss.
Intervening in a mindless universe,
Its message crept through the reluctant hush
Calling the adventure of consciousness and joy
And, conquering Nature's disillusioned breast,
Compelled renewed consent to see and feel.
A thought was sown in the unsounded Void,
A sense was born within the darkness' depths,
A memory quivered in the heart of Time
As if a soul long dead were moved to live:
But the oblivion that succeeds the fall,
Had blotted the crowded tablets of the past,
And all that was destroyed must he rebuilt
And old experience laboured out once more.
All can be done if the God-touch is there.

Savitri: Book I: canto 1, pp. 4-5.

Commentary

The Adventure of Consciousness

Because the Light was in the Dark, the Dark sought the Light. Because the Dark was in the Light, the Light sought the Dark. The hesitating hues of the Supramental Sun broke as the lids of the morning break out of the shadows of receding night. The eye of Deity from the dumb deeps looked upon the kingdom of nescience as a Ray in reconnaissance of the Sun. It saw the cosmic drowse of earth. It sought its spirit fallen from the sphere of the Bliss. Intervening in a mindless world of ignorance in secret messages, it woke the cry in the heart of the Nought to seek the skies of the Supermind. It sowed the seed of the Supramental Thought. It woke the Vision of the Supramental Light. At its quivering touch, earth recalled from buried memories of past incarnations its search for the Supermind. Once more it stayed its flight to search for the Supermental Ray. Once more it aspired to reach the fields of the Supermind. For all things can be done when the God-Light touches us to do it.

DETAILED NOTES

23. *Hesitating Hue*
The hesitating hue of the Supramental dawn.

24. *An eye of Deity*
The Supermind.

25. *Dumb Deeps*
The Abyss of Matter.

26. *The Sun*
The Supramental Light.

27. *Weary World*
The world of Matter groaning under the tyranny of the reign of Night.

28. *A Spirit*
The spirit of Matter.

29. *Too Fallen*
The fall of Matter from the plane of the Supermind sits the Mind of Night.

30. *Mindless Universe*
The material world drowned in the Asuric Night.

31. *Adventure of Consciousness*
The evolution of Mind into Supermind.

32. *Consent*
The consent of the Spirit of Earth to change into Supermind.

33. *A Thought*
The Supramental thought concealed in the Void of Matter.

34. *A Sense*
The Supramental vision hidden in the depths of darkness.

35. *A Memory*

Earth's memory of past incarnations in its attempted movement for transmutation from Mind into Supermind.

36. *Blotted*

The memories of past incarnations that fall below the threshold of earth's consciousness.

37. *Rebuilt*

The reconstruction of Supermind after destruction of the debris of Matter.

3

THE IMPERISHABLE'S TREAD

The Mother, the symbol of the Supreme Force, woke to the immortal task of regeneration.

A lonely splendour from the invisible goal
Almost was flung on the opaque Inane.
Once more a tread perturbed the vacant Vasts;
Infinity's centre, a Face of rapturous calm
Parted the eternal lids that open heaven;
A Form from far beatitudes seemed to near.
Ambassadress twixt eternity and change,
The Omniscient Goddess leaned across the breadths
That wrap the fated journeyings of the stars
And saw the spaces ready for her feet.
Once she half looked behind for her veiled sun,
Then thoughtful, went to her immortal work,
Earth felt the imperishable's passage close:
The waking ear of Nature heard her steps
And wideness turned to her its its limitless eye,
And scattered on sealed depths, her luminous smile
Kindled to fire the silence of the worlds.

Savitri : Book I : canto 1, pp. 6-7.

Commentary

The Supramental Descent into Earth

Because matter needs matter for its transfiguration into Supramental Light, from the region of the Creative Ray a material form drops into the kingdom of nescience. A face human, though Divine, breaks the lids of the higher heavens and falls into the fields of change. From the far beatitudes the Omniscient Goddess beheld the breadths of the lower heavens. She saw the fields of Time and Space beneath her feet ready for the Supramental Sun behind the veil of Matter and Mind. The sleeping earth hearing her footfall from slumber woke. In response the beam illumined all the fields of Matter, Mind and Life. But too brief for mortal's eyes was the immortal presence. Swift the Ray sped from Matter's realm to the Spaces of the Supramental Light.

DETAILED NOTES

38. *A lonely Splendour*
    The Single Ray of the Absolute.

39. *From the Invisible Goal*
    The regions of the Supermind.

40. *Opaque Inane*
    The kingdom of Matter.

41. *The Vacant Vasts*
    The fields of the worlds of the rare substances.

42. *Infinity's Centre*
    Supermind.

43. *A Face*
    The embodied Supermind.

44. *Ambassadress*
    Supermind.

45. *Twixt Eternity and Change*

Supermind which lies between the fields of the Absolute and the fields of Matter.

46. *The Omniscient Goddess*

The embodied Supermind.

47. *Her Veiled Sun*

The concealed Supermind.

48. *Kindled to Fire*

The Supramentalisation of the fields of Matter and Mind.

4

THE WITHDRAWAL

The Supreme Force withdrew behind the veils
to effect more potently the work of evolution.

Then the divine afflatus, spent, withdrew,
Unwanted, fading from the mortal's range,
A sacred yearning lingered in its trace,
The worship of a Presence and a Power.
Too perfect to be held by death-bound hearts,
The prescience of a marvellous birth to come.
Only a little the God-light can stay:
Spiritual beauty illumining human sight
Lines with its passion and mystery Matter's mask
And squanders eternity on a beat of Time.
As when a soul draws near the sill of birth,
Adjoining mortal time to Timelessness,
A spare of deity lost in Matter's crypt
Its lustre vanishes in the inconscient planes,
That transitory glow of magic fire
So now dissolved in bright accustomed air.
The message ceased and waned the messenger.
The single Call, the uncompanioned Power,

Drew back into some far-off secret world
The hue and marvel of the supernal beam.
Savitri: Book I: canto 1, pp. 7-8.

Commentary

The Evanishment of the Supramental Light from the Earth

The Supramental Light in its mastery of wisdom knowing that its long sojourn in Matter would destroy the kingdom of nescience, withdraws from the mortal range. Swift in her task and swift in her evanishment the Supernal retreats into the inconscient planes. Its magic fire dissolves. The messenger and the message recede from the range of the mortal lid.

DETAILED NOTES

49. *Withdrew*

The withdrawal of the Supramental Light into the depths of Matter.

50. *Matter's Mask*

Supermind that lies hid behind Matter's veil.

51. *A Spare of Deity*

Supermind concealed in Matter's depth.

52. *Inconscient Planes*

The planes of Matter.

53. *Secret World*

The concealed regions of the Supernal Being.

5

SAVITRI

Savitri, the incarnation of the Grace, takes her station in time to achieve earth-transfiguration.

All in her pointed to a nobler kind.
Near to earth's wideness, intimate with heaven,

Exalted and swift her young large-visioned spirit
Voyaging through worlds of splendour and of calm
Overflew the ways of thought to unborn things.
Ardent was her self-poised unstumbling will;
Her mind, a sea of white sincerity,
Passionate in flow, had not one turbid wave.
As in mystic and dynamic dance
A priestess of immaculate ecstasies
Inspired and ruled from Truth's revealing vault
Moves in some prophet cavern of the gods,
A heart of silence in the hands of joy
Inhabited with rich creative beats
A body like a parable of dawn
That seemed a niche for veiled divinity
Or golden temple door to things beyond.
Immortal rhythm swayed in her time-born steps;
Her look, her smile awoke celestial sense
Even in earth-stuff, and their intense delight
Poured a supernal beauty on men's lives.

Savitri: Book I: canto 2, pp. 18-19.

Commentary

The Incarnation of Savitri

The next descent of the Supramental Ray is not in a transient Light. For more durable action it appears in the incarnation of Savitri. Savitri, coming in answer to Aswapathy's prayer is born with a mortal body and a mortal mind. She is intimate with heaven and intimate with earth. Her body is the body of the material world, her mind is the mind of earth. But within her outer form in depths divine, secluded from sight, is the divinity of Supermind. The Supramental rhythm governs her body. Upon men's lives she sheds the radiance of the Supernal Beam.

DETAILED NOTES

54. *Near to Earth's Wideness*

The Supramental Light in Savitri is near to earth as it is enclosed in the body of earth.

55. *Intimate with Heaven*

The Supramental Light within her body is close to heaven. Savitri is the embodied Light of Supermind.

56. *Her Self*

The mortal self of Savitri ardent with the delight of the Supermind.

57. *Her Mind*

Her mind is formed with the radiant Light of Supermind and is as a sea of white sincerity and Truth.

58. *Not one Turbid Wave*

Not one turbid wave affects the mind of Savitri which is held in the unshakable poise of the Supermind.

59. *A Priestess*

Savitri is the ambassadress between Mind and Supermind and with her immaculate ecstasies supramentalises the field of Matter and Mind.

60. *A Body*

The body of Savitri is wrought of a Light free of the night of matter.

61. *Veiled Divinity*

Concealed Supermind.

62. *Immortals Rhythm*

The Supramental rhythm rules Savitri's time-born steps.

63. *Supernal Beauty*

The Supramental manifestation of beauty in Savitri.

6

ASWAPATHY

Aswapathy King of Madra, Savitri's father, commences the Yoga of ascent to the Supreme.

His was a spirit that stooped from larger spheres
Into our province of ephemeral sight,

A colonist from immortality.
A pointing beam of earth's uncertain roads,
His birth held up a symbol and a sign;
His human self like a translucent cloak
Covered the All-Wise who leads the unseeing world.
Affiliated to cosmic Space and Time
And paying here God's debt to earth and man
A greater sonship was his divine right.
Although consenting to mortal ignorance,
His knowledge shared the Light ineffable.
A strength of the original Permanence
Entangled in the moment and its flow,
He kept the vision of the Vasta behind:
A power was in him from the Unknowable.
As treasurer of superhuman dreams,
He bore the stamp of mighty memories
And shed their grandoise ray on human life.
His days were a long growth to the Supreme.
A skyward being nourishing its roots
On sustenance from occult spiritual founts
Climbed through white rays to meet an unseen Sun.

Savitri: Book I: canto 3, pp. 26-27.

Commentary

The Entanglement in Matter

As Savitri is the symbol of the descent of Supermind into Matter her father, Aswapathy is the symbol of the aspiration of the material mind to reach the realms of Supermind. Aswapathy is entangled in the mesh of substance. He is the symbol of the sigh of the mortal dust. He is the Spirit held in the shackles of the Mind of Night. Consenting to mortal ignorance beneath the cloak of Matter Mind and Life, he is the seeker of the Supramental Light. In his secret soul he bears memories of past incarnations in the search for the Supreme. His skyward being nourished by the roots of earth is on an ascendent flight to meet the Supramental Light.

DETAILED NOTES

64. *Spirit*

The concealed Supermind in Aswapathy.

65. *Ephemeral Sight*

The transitory plane of Matter.

66. *A Pointing Beam*

The Supramental Light illumining the darkened roads of Life.

67. *Cloak*

The cloak of Body, Mind and Life veiling the Supermind within.

68. *A Strength of the Original Permanence*

The Supermind entangled in the densities of Matter, Mind and Life.

69. *Growth*

The evolution from Mind to Supermind.

70. *White Rays*

The white Rays of the subtle fields of Matter opening to the vision of Supermind.

71. *Unseen Sun*

The Supermind.

7

ASWAPATHY'S YOGA

Aswapathy attained clairvoyancy by
which he saw the fields of the unseen.

The soul's experience of its deeper sheaths
No more slept drugged by Matter's dominance.
In the dead walls closing us from wider self,
Into a secrecy of apparent sleep,

The mystic tract beyond our waking thoughts,
A door parted, built in by Matter's force,
Releasing things unseized by earthly sense;
A world unseen unknown by outward mind
Appeared in the silent spaces of the soul.
He sat in secret chambers looking out
Into the luminous countries of the unborn
Where all things dreamed by the Mind are seen and true
And all that the life longs for is drawn close.
He saw the Perfect in their starry homes
Wearing the glory of a deathless form
Lain in the arms of the Eternal's peace,
Rapt in the heart-beats of God-ecstasy.
He lived in the mystic space where thought is born
And will is nursed by an ethereal Power
And fed on the white milk of the Eternal's strengths
Till it grows into the likeness of a god.

Savitri, Book I: canto 3, pp. 32-33.

Commentary

Aswapathy's ascent from mind to supermind

Out of subtle sheaths of the subtle substance, out of the drugged dominance of Matter, out of the dead walls of the Time and Space, Aswapathy in trance emerges upon the hidden expanses of the soul. The open lids of clairvoyance reveal the Supermind in the starry homes of the Light. In joy he enters the ethereal trance of the Supermind.

DETAILED NOTES

72. *Deeper Sheaths*

The hidden sheaths of subtle bodies and subtle worlds of the rare substance.

73. *Drugged*

The sleep of the Kingdom of Nescience.

74. *Dead Walls*

The enclosures of Body, Mind and Life which shut off the radiant Light of Supermind.

75. *The Mystic Tract*

The world of the Rare Substances.

76. *Releasing*

Releasing the powers of clairvoyance hidden in man.

77. *Silent Spaces*

The unseen breadths of the Supermind.

78. *Secret Chambers*

From the occult chambers of the inner mind Aswapathy explores the territory of the Supramental Light.

79. *Mystic Space*

The regions of the Supramental Light.

80. *An Ethereal Power*

The Supermind.

81. *It Grows*

The evolution from Mind to Supermind.

8

THE PLUNGE INTO THE INFINITE

Aswapathy passed beyond thought to the shoreless Infinite.

This huge material universe became
A small result of a stupendous force.
Overtaking the moment the eternal Ray
Illumined that which never yet was made
Thought lay down in a mighty voicelessness;
The toiling thinker widened and grew still,
Wisdom transcendent touched his quivering heart;
His soul could sail beyond thought's luminous bar;
Mind screened no more the shoreless infinite.
Across a void retreating sky he glimpsed
Through a last glimmer and drift of vanishing stars
The superconscient realms of motionless peace

Where judgment ceases and the world is mute
And the Unconceived lies pathless and alone.

Savitri: Book: canto 3, pp. 39.

Commentary

Aswapathy's Vision of the Super Conscient Realms

In a keener concentration of sensitivities Aswapathy passes beyond the material universe which in the broader theatre of the Supramental vision seems a puny point built by the stupendous Force. In pursuit of the Ray from field to field of the rare ascensions, the thought of Aswapathy loses all its voicefulness. The thinker widens into Spirit. With the smooth sails of the white transcendence he moves beyond the bars of thought. On his mind's screen appear the shoreless shores of the Absolute. Then in the last glimmer of the vanishing stars his dazzled lids beheld the superconscient realms of peace where thought and word are mute.

DETAILED NOTES

82. *Material Universe*

The world of Matter, Mind and Life.

83. *The Eternal Ray*

The Supermind.

84. *Thought*

Thought is silenced in the Supramental plane.

85. *Wisdom Transcendent*

The Supermind.

86. *Shoreless Infinite*

The endless fields of the Supermind.

87. *Super-Conscient Realms*

The fields of Supermind.

9

THE SPIRITUAL POISE

Aswapathy attained the poise of the Integral Yoga.
At last was won a firm spiritual poise,
A constant lodging in the Eternal's realm,
A safety in the Silence and the Ray,
A settlement in the Immutable.
His heights of being lived in the still Self;
His mind could rest on a supernal ground
And look down on the magic and the play
Where the God-child lies on the lap of Night and Dawn
And the Everlasting puts on Time's disguise.
To the Still heights and to the troubled depths
His equal spirit gave its vast assent:
A poised serenity of tranquil strength,
A wide unshaken look on Time's unrest
Faced all experience with unaltered peace.

Savitri: Book I: canto 3, pp. 41-42.

Commentary

The Constant Lodging in the Supermind

Changed by the Yoga of the ascent, Aswapathy's Spirit has a constant lodging in the Light. The King lives in the safety and the silence of the Ray. In the still heights, Time throws off all its veils. The troubled ways of Matter, Mind and Life lose their turbulence. A wide and unshaken look faces all the terrors of experience. For terror and tears are exiles in the Supramental air.

DETAILED NOTES

88. *Spiritual Poise*

The spiritual station of the soul of Aswapathy in the Supramental Light.

89. *A Constant Lodging*

A firm position in the Supramental Light free of ascents and descents from or to the Ray.

90. *A Safety*
In the fields of the Supramental where no fear is ensconced.

91. *Silence*
The hushed air of the Supermind.

92. *Still Self*
The Supermind.

93. *Time's Disguise*
The veils of Matter, Mind and Life.

94. *Unshaken Look*
The look of the detached Supermind.

10

CONCENTRATION

Aswapathy's meditation led him to the heights of trance.

All-vision gathered into a single ray,
As when the eyes stare at an invisible point
Till through the intensity of one luminous spot
An apocalypse of a world of images
Enters into the kingdom of the seer.
A great nude arm of splendour suddenly rose;
It rent the gause opaque of Nescience:
Her lifted finger's keen unthinkable tip
Bared with a stab of flame the closed Beyond.
An eye awake in voiceless heights of trance,
A mind plucking at the unimaginable,
Overleaping with a sole and perilous bound
The high black wall hiding superconscience,
She broke in with inspired speech for scythe
And plundered the Unknowable's vast estate.

Savitri: Book I: canto 3, p. 45.

Commentary

The Meditative Vision of Aswapathy

As one in meditative trance gazes upon a concentrated point which breaks into light and reveals a world of images in a single glance, so Aswapathy in stillness entered into the kingdom of the seer. Before his eyes stood Supermind's single Ray rending the webs of Nescience. The Goddess of the Omniscient Light Lifted the veils of Matter, Mind and Life. From subtleties of trance he saw the heights of trance, His mind raced beyond the bounds of mind and destroyed the walls of Matter which hide the fields of Supermind.

DETAILED NOTES

95. *All-Vision*

The Cosmic Perception.

96. *Single Ray*

The unitarian Consciousness of Supermind.

97. *Luminous Spot*

The point of concentration.

98. *Nude Arm*

The form of the Supramental Light.

99. *Nescience*

The world of Matter.

100. *The Closed Beyond*

The hidden fields of Supermind.

101. *An Eye Awake*

The lids awakened in clairvoyance.

102. *A Mind*

The aspiring Mind of Aswapathy seeking the undreamed of worlds of Supermind.

103. *Black Wall*

The dark wall of Matter holding in concealment the Supramental Ray.

104. *Hiding Superconscience*

The Supermind hid in Matter's cell.

11
OVERMIND

Moving from the fields of Luminous and Intuitive mind, Aswapathy climbed to the shimmering ridge of Overmind in preparation for the ascent into Supermind.

The immobile lips, the great surreal wings,
The visage masked by superconscient Sleep,
The eyes with their closed lids that see all things,
Appeared of the Architect who builds in trance.
The original Desire born in the Void
Peered out; he saw the Hope that never sleeps,
The feet that run behind a fleeting fate,
The ineffable meaning of the endless dream.
As if a torch held by a power of God,
The radiant world of the everlasting Truth
Glimmered like a faint star bordering the night
Above the golden Overmind's shimmering ridge.

Savitri: Book I: canto 3, p. 47.

Commentary

Aswapathy's Passage into Overmind

From the fields of the Mind of Night and the Intuitive Mind, passing through the doors of the Mind of Light Aswapathy reaches the shimmering ridges of the Overmind which beckon to the realms of Supermind. Before his closed lids appears the Face of the Architect who builds all the worlds of trance. He sees the fields of original desire born of the void. He beholds the form of hope that never dies. In the finest glance he cons the hieroglyphics of the mystery of Matter. From the Overmind he kens the world of the Mind of Night below and with the upward gaze he views the distant ranges of the Supermind.

DETAILED NOTES

105. *Immobile Lips*

The appearance of the Absolute Light in form.

106. *The Visage Masked*

The veiled Face of the Absolute.

107. *The Architect*

The Uncreated Ray.

108. *Original Desire*

The original desire which draws the soul into many incarnations in earth.

109. *The Radiant World*

The faint star of the Supermind in glimmering in distance beyond the rays of the Overmind.

110. *Overminds Shimmering Ridge*

The Overmental plane which is the link between the Mind of Night and the Knot of Matter below and the Mind of Supermind above.

12

THE ABSOLUTE SPIRIT

In the supreme rapture Aswapathy
sees the Ray of the Absolute Self

In the wide signless ether of the Self,
In the unchanging Silence white and nude,
Aloof, resplendent like gold dazzling suns
Veiled by the Ray no mortal eye can hear,
The Spirit's free and absolute potencies
Burned in the solitude of the thoughts of God.

A rapture and a radiance and a hush
Delivered from the approach of wounded hearts,
Denied to the Idea that looks at grief,
Remote from the Force that cries out in its pain,
In his inalianable bliss they live.
Immaculate in a self-knowledge and self-power,
Calm they repose on the eternal Will.

Savitri: Book I: canto 4, p. 65

Commentary

The Ascent of Aswapathy into the Fields of the Absolute

Ascending from the worlds of Overmind and Supermind Aswapathy reaches the field of the Uncreated Ray. There where the beams of the Absolute burn in the solitudes of God, in the signless ether of God's being Aswapathy meets the Absolute Bliss. There no grief comes and no pain cries from the worlds of Matter, Mind and Life.

DETAILED NOTES

111. *Signless Ether*
The rare air of the Absolute.

112. *Dazzling Suns*
The dazzling suns of the Supermind veiled by the Absolute Ray.

113. *A Radiance*
The Absolute Radiance of the Uncreated Ray.

114. *Delivered*
A Absolute Spirit free from the wounds of the world of Matter, Mind and Life.

115. *Bliss*
The Bliss of the Absolute.

116. *Self Knowledge*
The Pure Consciousness of the Absolute.

117. *Self Power*
The Conscious Force of the Absolute.

13

EARTH'S TRANSFIGURATION

In the hush of the Divine, the Human soul meets the Perfect and the Alone.

The Absolute, the Perfect, the Alone
Has called out of the Silence his mute Force
Where she lay in the featureless and formless hush
Guarding from Time by her immobile sleep
The ineffable puissance of his solitude.
The Absolute, the Perfect, the Alone
Has entered with his silence into space;
He has fashioned these countless persons of one self;
He lives in all, who lived in his Vast alone;
Space is himself and Time is only he.
The Absolute, the Perfect the Immune,
One who is in us our secret self,
Our mask of imperfection has assumed,
He has made this tenement of flesh his own,
His image in the human measure cast
That to his divine measure we might rise;
Then in a figure of divinity
The Maker shall recast us and impose
A plan of godhead on the mortal's mould
Lifting our finite minds to his infinite,
Touching the moment with eternity.
This transfiguration is earth's due to heaven:
A mutual debt binds man to the Supreme;
His nature we must put on as he put ours;
We are sons of God and must be even as he.

Savitri: Book I: canto 4, pp. 76-77

Commentary

The Secrets of the Self

Beyond the summits of the Supermind, Aswapathy passes into the kingdom of the Truth. In the Supramental consciousness he seizes the supreme truth of all being. The mute Force of the

Absolute he sees. The countless forms of the Ray he knows. All the mysteries of life are solved. The Absolute lives in all the fields of the Self. Man He is and God He is. Space He is and Time He is. The Secret Self He is and the revealed Self He is. Perfection He is and the Mask of Perfection He is. Flesh He is and the Spirit He is. A godly plan hath God designed the transfiguration of Matter, Mind and Life into Supermind.

DETAILED NOTES

118. *The Absolute*
The uncreated Ray.

119. *Formless Hush*
The hush in the fields of the Uncreated Ray.

120. *Mute Force*
The Supramental Light.

121. *Countless Persons*
All the children of the Uncreated Ray.

122 *Space*
The field of the Uncreated Ray.

123. *Time*
The moments of the Supramental Manifestation.

124. *Secret Self*
The Uncreated Ray in Matter, Mind and Life.

125. *Mask of Imperfection*
The mask of the Uncreated Ray in the field of Matter, Mind and Life.

126. *A Plan of Godhead*
The Supramentalisation of Matter, Mind and Life.

127. *Transfiguration*
The transformation of Matter, Mind and Life into Supermind.

128. *His Nature*

The super-nature of the Uncreated Ray.

129. *Sons of God*

The children of the earth destined to be transformed into the children of the Supermind.

14

THE MYSTIC VOYAGE

Led by the force of the Supreme Matter, the Human soul makes her voyage through mystic seas.

In the hidden strength of her omnipotent Will,
Driven by her breath across life's tossing deep,
Through the thunder's roar and through the windless hush,
Through fog and mist where nothing more is seen,
He carries her sealed orders in his breast.
Late will he know, opening the mystic script,
Whether to a blank part in the Unseen
He goes, or armed with her fiat, to discover
A new mind and body in the city of God
And enshrine the Immortal in his glory's house
And make the finite one with Infinity.
Across the salt waste of the endless years
Her ocean winds impel his errant boat,
The cosmic waters plashing as he goes,
A rumour around him and danger and a call.
Always he follows in her force's wake.
He sails through life and death and other life,
He travels on through waking and through sleep.
A power is on him from her occult force
That ties him to his own creations: fate,
And never can the mighty traveller rest
And never can the mystic voyage cease,
Till the nescient dusk is lifted from man's soul
And the morns of God have evertaken his night.

Savitri : Book I : Canto 4, p. 82

Commentary

The Voyage through the Seas of Nescience

The great gales of the Supermind drives the boat of the soul across the un-charted seas of nescience.. Fog and mist lay upon the waters. Thunder rolled in the sky above, and lightening spilled its flashes upon the turbulent ocean of the nought. But from the windless hush came a hidden voice summoning the soul to read the secret script of the fate written in the hollows of the heart. Whether the bark was going the soul knew not. Blank was the port and invisible the shore. Around her she heard a danger and a call. In the salt waste was the moan of the Spirit for the Light. The Force Occult heard the soul's prayer. It stilled the waves. It broke the surf, it showed to the soul in the sealed cavern of her being the sure futurity, the transformation of the soul's being into Light. Never did the Supramental Force rest, never did the mystic voyage over the ignorant seas pause, till it had lifted the nescient dusk from the soul. In the new body and in the new mind, in the city of the Supernal Being, the Spirit found its repose.

DETAILED NOTES

130. *Driven*
The hurricane of the Supramental Force.

131. *Thunder's*
The veil of the Supramental Light.

132. *The Mystic script*
The hieroglyphics of the Supermind.

133. *A new Mind and Body*
The Supramental Mind and Body.

134. *City of God*
The city of the Supermind.

135. *Finite one with Infinity*
The Supermind lifts the veil of the finite and reveals the infinite in the finite.

136. *Her Force*
The Supramental Light.

137. *The Mystic Voyage*
The voyage from Nescience to the Supermind.

138. *The Nescient Dusk*
The twilight of matter.

139. *Morns of God*
The Supramental Light over-coming the Night of the Asuras.

15

THE ASCENT

Aswapathy's aspiration, like a cone of fire, blazed to the heights of the Infinite till he was clothed with the garb of the supernature exceeding thought.

The Silence was his sole companion left.
Impassive he lived immune from earthly hopes,
A figure in the ineffable Witness' shrine
Packing the vast cathedral of his thoughts
Under its arches dim with infinity
And heavenward brooding of invisible wings.
A call was on him from intangible heights;
Indifferent to the little outpost Mind,
He dwelt in the wideness of the Eternal's reign.
His being now exceeded thinkable Space,
His boundless thought was neighbour to cosmic sight:
A universal light was in his eyes,
A golden influx flowed through heart and brain;
A force came down into his mortal limbs,
A current from eternal seas of Bliss;
He felt the invasion and the nameless joy.
Aware of his occult omnipotent Source,
Allured by the conscient Ecstasy,

A living centre of the Illimitable
Widened to equate with the world's circumference,
He turned to his immense spiritual fate.
Abandoned on a canvas of torn air,
A picture lost in far and fading streaks,
The earth-nature's summits sank below his feet.
He climbed to meet the infinite more above.
The immobile's ocean-silence saw him pass,
An arrow leaping through eternity
Suddenly shot from the tense bow of Time,
A ray returning to its parent sun.
Opponent of that glory of escape
The black inconscient swung its dragon tail
Lashing a slumberous Infinite by its force
Into the deep obscurities of form :
Death lay beneath him like a gate of sleep.
One-pointed to the immaculate Delight,
Questing for God as for a splended pray,
He mounted burning like a cone of fire.

Savitri: Book I : canto 5, pp. 89-90

Commentary

The call of the Heights

Aswapathy's spirit hears the call of the heights. It springs, as an arrow springs, from the bow to the mark of the still Absolute. From the vast cathedral of human thought, from the dim parks and passages of the mind, it leaps to the infinite. Below the king is the outpost of mind diminished and dwarfed from his station in cosmic sight. The sureate flood of the Supramental light bathes his heart and brain. The current of the Supramental force invades all portions of his being. In the arms of the ecstasies his personality is enlarged. He becomes a living centre of the Infinite Light widening to embrace all the worlds of the subtle substances. Donning the robes of the super-nature, he loses sight of the hill and dales of the earth-nature. He climbs grade after grade into the secret summits of the Infinite Light. Around him in subtle circumambient air, the oceanic silences of the vast, he ascends to the supramental peaks. The mortal ray returns to the immortal sun. But in every tread of his ascensions there is the drag of inconscient matter impeding the Supramental ascent. Death loses its perils For death is a sleep of a rare awakening into the fields of the immaculate delight. Burning as a cone of fire Aswapathy's soul arrives in the kingdom of the illumined Fire.

DETAILED NOTES

140. *Cathedral of his Thoughts*

The temple of Mortal Thought is not illumined. It is dim with the promise of the Light. An outpost of mind, the whole kingdom of Mind sinks into insignificance in the clasp of unthinkable space.

141. *A Golden Influx*

The descent of the Supramental Light into the body of Aswapathy.

142. *A Living Centre*

Human personality limits the psychic quest. It hides the large ranges of the super-nature. In the Supramental change the personality is exceeded. The soul lives as an individual centre of the Absolute Being.

143. *A Ray*

From the Supramental station the soul is not seen embodied in matter. For its true nature is not material. Matter is a mask. Substance is the Ray returning to its parent and source the Supramental Sun.

144. *The Black Inconscient*

But in the ascent from Matter to Supermind the black inconscient obstructs the flight of the human spirit. But the Forces of darkness are the secret Forces of the light. The speed of the spirit's flight is increased by delays which stabilise the evolution of the soul to Supermind.

16

THE DESCENT OF FORCE

The descent of the Suprament Force seized the King. He exceeded the nature of the ego and became the instrument of the Universal Self.

A Might, a Flame,
A Beauty half-visible with deathless eyes,
A violent ecstasy, a sweetness dire,
Enveloped him with its stupendous limbs
And penetrated nerve and heart and brain
That thrilled and fainted with the epiphany:
His nature shuddered in the Unknown's grasp.
In a moment shorter than Death, longer than Time,
By a power more ruthless than Love, happier than Heaven,
Taken sovereignty into eternal arms,
Haled and coerced by a stark absolute bliss,
In a whirlwind circuit of delight and force
Hurried into unimaginable depths,
Upborne into immeasurable heights,
It was torn out from its mortality
And underwent a new and bourneless change
An Omniscient knowing without sight or thought,
An indecipherable Omnipotence,
A mystic Form that could contain the worlds,
Yet make one human breast its passionate shrine,
Drew him out of his seeking loneliness
Into the magnitudes of God's embrace.
As when a timeless Eye annuls the hours
Abolishing the agent and the act,
So new his spirit shone out wide, blank, pure:
His wakened mind became an empty slate
On which the Universal and Sole could write.

Savitri: Book I: canto 5, p. 92

Commentary

The Unknown's Grasp

In a subtle seeking the Supramental Force, in a pause briefer than death and larger than Time with a ruthless love, in a whirlwind of delight, hales the King into the depths of unimaginable Light. Transmuting the body and the Mind of Aswapathy, it breaks up all the walls of the mortal being. The Timeless Eye of God annuls all the schedules of the human hours. The Spirit of Aswapathy awakened widening into the breadths of the Divine embrace.

DETAILED NOTES

145. *Enveloped*

The Supermind is the All-Eye. It touches the nerve, the heart, the brain of Aswapathy with the epiphany of the Absolute Ray.

146. *The Unknown's Grasp*

The grip of the Supramental Light upon Body, Mind and Life effecting the Supramental Change.

147. *Whirlwind*

The currents of the Supramental Ray hurry the Spirit of Aswapathy into the immeasurable distances and depths of the Supermind.

148. *Bourneless Change*

The change of the Mind, Body and Matter into the Supramental Light.

149. *A Mystic Form*

The embodied form of the Supramental Light.

150. *God's Embrace*

The Divine touch upon the flesh showing the gleams of the skies of the Divine.

151. *An Empty Slate*

All the illusions born of Mind, Matter and Life, are erased by the Hand Divine. Aswapathy's being, outer and inner, is cleaned of all impurities which bar the vision of the Absolute.

17

THE ESCAPE

Aswapathy, breaking the ring of the ego and the triple cord of body, Mind and Life, beheld the hidden Absolute.

Eternity's contact broke the mould of sense.
A greater force than the earthly held his limbs,
Huge workings bared his undiscovered sheaths,
Strange energies wrought and screened tremendous hands
Unwound the triple cord of mind and freed
The heavenly wideness of a Godhead's gaze.
As through a dress the wearer's shape is seen,
There reached through forms to the hidden absolute
A cosmic feeling and transcendent sight.
Increased and heightened were the instruments.
Illusion lost her aggrandising lens;
As from her failing hand the measures fell,
Atomic looked the things that loomed so large.
The little ego's ring could join no more;
In the enormous spaces of the self
The body now seemed only a wandering shell,
His mind the many-frescoed outer court
Of an imperishable Inhabitant:
His spirit breathed a superhuman air.
The imprisoned deity rent its magic fence
As with a sound of thunder and of seas,
Vast barriers crashed around the huge escape.

Savitri: Book I: canto 5, p. 95

Commentary

The Liberation From the Bonds of Physical Being

The Light of the Supermind dissolves all the resistances of the lower being. It frees the Spirit of Aswapathy from the triple cords of Matter, Mind and Life. It widens his embrace of the heavenly domains behind the veil. Through the masks of mind Aswapathy's Spirit beholds the Spirit. For the Supramental Beam heightened all the instruments of Aswapathy's being. In the transmutation all illusion's aggrandising lens lose their hold.

Atomic seem the things that appear so large to the mental gazing. All the rings of the ego are broken by the Ray. The body appears a vesture worn and shed. Mind appears as the outer realm of the inner Supermind. The imperishable spirit is loosened from the subtle sheaths of the subtle bodies. The imprisoned Divinity within Aswapathy rends the magic fence of Body, Mind and Life. The barriers of matter break. The soul of Aswapathy has its escape from the hold of Matter.

DETAILED NOTES

152. *Undiscovered Sheaths*

The Spirit of Aswapathy is veiled in several sheaths of invisible bodies. The first sheath is the Astral body of invisible matter; the second, the mental body of rare substances; and third, the Causal body on the borders of the Formless Ray. The physical body is the instrument of Matter. The astral body is the instrument of Astral Life. The Mental Body is the instrument of the mental life; The Causal body is the instrument of the formless life. Each body is an instrument of evolution. The Supramental evolution is beyond the evolution of the bodies. It is the evolution of the Spirit and not the evolution of the form.

153. *The Triple Cord*

The triple cords of Body, Mind and Life are the bonds which imprison the soul within.

154. *The Hidden Absolute*

The Supramental Light veiled within the shells of Matter, Mind and Life.

155. *Ego's Ring*

The ring of Matter, Mind and Life constitute the bonds of the lower being. The Supramental Light breaks all the chains of the material being.

156. *The Imperishable Inhabitant*

The veiled Absolute within the womb of Matter, Mind and Life.

157. *The Imprisoned Deity*

The subtle Supramental Light within the outer forms of Matter, Mind and Life.

158. *The Huge Escape*

The liberation from the fetters of Matter, Mind and Life wrought by the Supramental Ray.

18

THE TRIUNE ECSTASIES

Aswapathy in the state of supreme ecstasy
fell at the stupendous gates of the Alone.

A paean swelled from the lost musing deeps;
An anthem pealed to the triune ecstasies,
A cry of the moments to the Immortal's bliss.
As if the strophes of cosmic ode,
A hierarchy of climbing harmonies
Peopled with voices and with visages
Aspired in a crescendo of the Gods
From Matter's abysses to the Spirit's peaks.
Above were the Immortal's changeless, seats,
White chambers of dalliance with Eternity
And the stupendous gates of the Alone.

Savitri: Book I: canto 5, p. 130

Commentary

The Gates of the Alone

Aswapathy's climb into the harmonies of the Divine is through graded ascent. He arises from matter's abyss to the peaks of the Spirit through the Mind of Light, Overmind and the Supermind. From the fields of Supermind be confronts the doors of the Alone in the fields of the Triune Ecstasies.

DETAILED NOTES

159. *The Triune Ecstasies*

In the map of the ascent as disclosed in the several

chapters of "The Life Divine" there are three points of the ascensions. First is the ascension from the Mind of Night and Knot of Matter into the Mind of Light; Second the ascension from Overmind to Supermind. The ascension from the Mind of Night to Supermind is called by Sri Aurobindo the Lower Hemisphere of the Divine Life. Thirdly, beyond the fields of the Supermind are the triple fields of the Triune Ecstasies the region of the Absolute Consciousness—SACHCHIDANANDA. The Triune Ecstasies in Christian scripture are called the Holy Trinity from which descend all the fields of light. In the Hindu scriptures the Triune Ecstasies are termed Sachchidananda, the Conscious Force, the Conscious Existence and the Conscious Delight of the Absolute. In theosophy the Triune Ecstasies are named the Triple Logos. In the Integral Yoga the Absolute experience is called the experience of the Triune Ecstasies.

160. *Matter's Abysses*

The fields of the Lower Trilogy. The Upper Trilogy is the field of the Triune Ecstasies.

161. *The Spirit's Peaks*

The peaks of the Mind of Light, Overmind and Supermind.

162. *The Gates of the Alone*

The fields of the Triune Ecstasies.

19

THE SUMMIT

Aswapathy mounted the bare Summit of Creation.

Apart in an unfathomed loneliness,
He travelled in his mute and single strength
Bearing the burden of the world's desire.

A formless Stillness called a nameless Light.
Above him was the white immobile Ray.
Around him the eternal Silences.
No term was fixed to the high-pitched attempt;
World after world disclosed its guarded powers,
Heaven after heaven its deep beatitudes,
But still the invisible Magnet drew his soul.
A figure sole on Nature's giant stair,
He mounted towards an indiscernible end
On the bare summit of created things.

Savitri: Book II: canto 1, pp. 114-15.

20

THE KINGDOMS OF BEATITUDE

Aswapathy arrives at the hidden kingdom of Bliss.

As through a magic television's glass
Outlined to some magnifying inner eye
They shone like images thrown from a far scene
Too high and glad for mortal lids to seize.
But near and real to the longing heart
And to the body's passionate thought and sense
Are the hidden kingdoms of beatitude.
In some close unattained realm which yet we feel,
Immune from the harsh clutch of Death and Time,
Escaping the search of sorrow and desire,
In bright enchanted safe peripheries
For ever wallowing in bliss they lie.

Savitri: Book II, canto 3, p. 135

Commentary

The Safe Peripheries of the Bliss

As on a television screen, in a magnified radiance, open for Aswapathy the last fields of the Bliss. Where Space and Time lose their clutch in a Sphere of guarded bliss, the soul of Aswapathy reposes.

DETAILED NOTES

167. *Television's Glass*

In the flourish of the Supramental clairvoyance the lids of Aswapathy behold the sealed realms of the Bliss.

168. *Safe Peripheries*

The Sphere of the Bliss is guarded by spirits from the Assaults of the Asuric powers.

21

THE SERPENT FORCE

Aswapathy contacted the Force of the superconscient Kundalini.

The first writhings of the cosmic Serpent Force
Uncoiled from the mystic ring of Matter's trance;
It raised its head in the warm air of life.
It could not cast off yet Night's suffering sleep
Or wear as yet mind's wonder-flecks and streaks,
Put on its jewelled hood the crown of soul
Or stand erect in the blaze of spirit's sun.
As yet were only seen foulness and force,
The secret crawl of consciousness to light
Through a fertile slime of lust and battening sense,
Beneath the body's crust of thickened self
A tardy fervent working in the dark,
The turbid yeast of Nature's passionate change,
Ferment of the soul's creation out of mire.

Savitri: Book II, canto 4, pp. 155-56

Commentary

The Crawl of the Serpent Force to the Light

The spirit of Aswapathy sees the writhing of the material force of the Kundalini. Secretly it lies asleep in matter's base. The veiled Kundalini—the universal cosmic force—awakens to the impact of the Supramental Ray. It resists the pressure of the

Light. Struck by the Supramental shine it crawls out of Matter into Light.

Detailed Notes

169. *Serpent Force*

The symbol of the Material Force.

170. *Ring of Matter*

The Rings of Matter, Mind and Life shut out the Supramental Light.

171. *The Secret Crawl*

The evolutionary advance of the physical consciousness towards the Supramental Light.

22

APPEARANCE

Matter disappeared and became an ocean of electrical Energy, a field of Appearance whirled by Invisible Forces.

At first was only an etheric Space:
Its huge vibrations circled round and round
Housing some unconceived initiative:
Upheld by a supreme original Breath
Expansion and contraction's mystic act
Created touch and friction in the void.
Into abstract emptiness brought clash and clasp:
Parent of an expanding universe
In a matrix of disintegrating force,
By spending it conserved an endless sum.
On the hearth of Space it kindled a viewless Fire
That, scattering worlds as one might scatter seeds,
Whirled out the luminous order of the stars.
An ocean of electric Energy
Formlessly formed its strange wave-particles
Constructing by their dance this solid scheme.
Its mightiness in the atom shut to rest,

Masses were forged or feigned and visible shapes:
Light flung the photon's swift revealing spark
And showed, in the minuteness of its flash
Imaged, this cosmos of apparent things.

Savitri: Book II, Canto 5, pp. 175-76

Commentary

The World of Apparent Things

The clairvoyant eye of Aswapathy seeks to probe the apparent matter. First it beholds emptiness. Within etheric space it finds the worlds of vibration. Within the fields of vibration it sees the viewless fire. It apprehends the notion of an electric energy. It watches the wave particles of matter consolidating the whole field of the material manifestation. It views the potencies of the atom. It marks the light particles of the material energies.

DETAILED NOTES

172. *Etheric Space*

This is the ether-hypothesis of Science, within which the Material Life moves.

173. *Vibrations*

These are the vibrations which Science conjectures as the motion in the Field of Matter.

174. *Expanding Universe*

This is the expanding universe of modern Science in respect of the movements of matter.

175. *Viewless Fire*

The Supramental Light as yet unknown to Science.

176. *Electric Energy*

The force of electricity in matter of which Science has no full conception. From the view of spiritual realisation the electrical energy is the Force of the Supermind.

177. *Wave Particles*

According to Science Matter has a double aspect: Wave and Particle. In the Particle aspect Matter is hard within the fields of Space and Time. In the wave aspect Matter is immaterial, outside the fields of Space and Time.

178. *The Atom*

The reference is to nuclear energy asleep in matter's crypt. Its fission releases the nuclear blast.

179. *Apparent Things*

The whole field of Science is based upon conjecture of the mind and does not touch the real. The same data of Science is the search for the surface of things. Deep within the moulds of sense is hidden the Light of Supermind.

23

THE DEEPER MYSTERY

Aswapathy realised the deeper mystery—the witnessing soul behind body and mind—seeking a transformation into the Supernature.

All is not here a blinded Nature's task:
A word, a Wisdom watches us from on high,
A Witness sanctioning her will and works,
An Eye unseen in the unseeing vast;
There is an Influence from a Light above,
There are thoughts remote and sealed eternities:
A mystic motive drives the stars and suns.
In this passage from a deaf unknowing Force
To struggling consciousness and transient breath
A mighty supernature waits on Time.
The world is other than we now think and see,
Our lives a deeper mystery than we have dreamed;

Savitri: Book II, Canto 5, p. 191

Commentary

The Mighty Supernature

Aswapathy's Spirit realises the work of the stupendous Supernature beneath the world of apparent Matter. Within Aswapathy is the detached and witnessing soul free of the illusions of Matter and Mind. From the Supramental poise Aswapathy sees the deeper mysteries of apparent things.

DETAILED NOTES

180. *Nature's Task*

Nature's task does not belong to a blind domain. For its work is of wisdom that watches from above.
Nature is the secret Supermind.

181. *A Witness*

There is within our being a witnessing consciousness which sees the world without the world's illusions. The detached consciousness is the consciousness of the Supermind fully cognisant of both the worlds of reality and the worlds of the illusion.

182. *Sealed Eternities*

The secret worlds of Supermind held in the heart of the Supramental Light.

183. *Supernature*

The Supermind which in the progress of evolving Time brings to birth all the phases of the Supramental Manifestation.

24

DEATH

A sombre mystery lays its hand on Aswapathy—the finger of Death.

Then from the sombre mystery of the gulfs
And from the hollow bosom of the Mask
Something crept forth that seemed a shapeless Thought.

A fatal Influence upon creatures stole
Whose lethal touch pursued the immortal spirit.
On life was laid the hunting finger of Death
And overcast with error, grief and pain
The soul's native will for truth and joy and light.
A deformation coiled that claimed to be
The being's very turn, Nature's true drive.
A hostile and pervading Mind at work
In every corner ensconced of conscious life
Corrupted Truth with her own formulas;
Intercepter of the listening of the soul,
Afflicting knowledge with the hue of doubt
It captured the oracles of the occult gods.
Effaced the signposts of Life's pilgrimage,
Cancelled the firm rock-edicts graved by Time,
And on the foundations of the cosmic Law
Erected its bronze pylons of misrule.

Savitri: Book II: canto. 7. p. 230.

Commentary

The Lethal Touch

The aspiring soul of Aswapathy now encounters the first struggle with the Dark. From the sombre mystery of matter, from the unillumined abyss of the inconscient, a sinister shadow steals to snare the soul in the net of Death. A lethal touch pursues the Spirit. It overcasts with clouds the gentle earth. With dim fingers it obliterates the Light. It appears as Nature's main drive in the field of Matter and Mind. Truth it corrupts.

The voice of the soul it hinders. Knowledge it mixes with a doubt. The oracles of Divinity it begins to deliver. The hostile force of the Asura seeks to abolish the Life Divine. It cancels the edicts of Time and on the floor of the inconscient it erects the edifice of Falsehood.

DETAILED NOTES

184. *The Lethal Touch*

The touch of Death is not real. It is the construction of the Mind testing the strength of the Spirit.

185. *Corrupted Truth*

As the figure of Death is a falsehood it has no abiding. The Shadows of Yama are dissolved by the illuminations of the Supermind.

186. *Effaced*

The effacement of life is apparent and not real. Behind the mask of Death is the power of the Supramental Light.

187. *Mis-Rule*

The mis-rule of the hostile Forces is broken by Light.

25

THE SONS OF DARKNESS

Aswapathy from the heights of Bliss descended by steps into the depths of the dark.

Opponents of the Highest they have come
Out of their world of soulless thought and power
To serve by enmity the cosmic scheme
Night is their refuge and strategic base.
Against the sword of Flame, the luminous Eye.
Bastioned they live in massive forts of gloom,
Calm and secure in sunless privacy:
No wandering ray of Heaven can enter there.
Armoured, protected by their lethal masks,
As in a studio of creative Death
The giant sons of Darkness sit and plan
The drama of the earth, their tragic stage.
All who would raise the fallen world must come
Under the dangerous arches of their power;
For even the radiant children of the gods
To darken their privilege is and dreadful right,
None can reach heaven who has not passed through hell.

Savitri: Book II, Canto 8, pp. 256-257

Commentary

The Opponents of the Most High

The Forces of Darkness dwell in sunless privacy in the limbo of the nether hell. No ray of heaven visits them. The lethal mask of Death they wear to affright the sons of mortality. In dens of Death they prepare the plans of Death. All the aspirants of the Ray must pass under the dangerous arches of Yama. For the sons of Darkness by enmity serve the Cosmic scheme.

DETAILED NOTES

188. *Opponents*
The hostile forces are the forces of the Light. By the work of the Dark they serve the designs of the Light.

189. *Forts of Gloom*
The pits of hell.

190. *Sons of Darkness*
The Asuric forces.

191. *Hell*
Hell is the first step to Paradise.

26

THE DESCENT INTO THE SUB-CONSCIENT

Aswapathy sounded the waters of the Subconscient.

He sounded the mystery dark and bottomless
of the enormous and unmeaning deeps
Whence struggling life in a dead universe rose.
There in the stark identity lost by mind
He felt the sealed sense of the insensible world
And a mute wisdom in the unknowing Night.
Into the abysmal secrecy he came
Where darkness peers from her mattress, grey and nude,
And stood on the last looked subconscient's floor

Where Being slept unconscious of its thoughts
And built the world not knowing what it built.

Savitri: Book II. Canto 8, pp. 261-262

Commentary

The Abysmal Secrecy

The Spirit of Aswapathy sounds the last mysteries of the Dark. In the Abysmal secrecies of matter, all Light is lost. The shadows of the Asuras peer from the corners of obscurity. The floor of the subconscient lies apparently unconscious and dead. But within it is still vibrant the Light of Supermind.

DETAILED NOTES

192. *The Mystery*
The Mystery of Mind, Matter and Life.

193. *The Insensible World*
The unconscious field of Matter.

194. *The Abysmal Secrecy*
The secrecy of Supermind concealed in Matter.

195. *Sub-Conscient's Floor*
The floor of unconscious matter where all being is asleep.

27

ABYSMS OF BLISS

From the gates of Hell Aswapathy rose to abysms of beauty.

As one who sees in the World-Magician's glass
A miracled imagery of soul-scapes flee
He traversed scenes of an immortal joy
And gazed into abysms of beauty and bliss.
Around him was a light of conscious suns
And a brooding gladness of great symbol things;
To meet him crowded plains of brilliant calm,

Mountains and violet valleys of the Blest,
Deep glens of joy and crooning waterfalls
And woods of quivering purple solitude.

Savitri: Book II, Canto 9, p. 265

Commentary

The Violet Valleys

The soul of Aswapathy passes from the smoke of hell into the violet valleys of the Bliss. In the abysms of the Light brood every shade or shape of gladness. Hills of every hue, glens of every joy, singing fountains and leaf of quivering woods, satisfy every cell of the ascending Spirit.

DETAILED NOTES

196. *Abysms of Beauty*

The scenes and sights of the plane of the Bliss.

197. *Violet Valleys*

The variegated hues of the fields of the Bliss.

28

MUSIC

Aswapathy became clairaudient and heard the music of the spheres.

Amid miraculous scents and wonder-hues
He met the forms that divinise the sight,
To music that can immortalise the Mind
And make the heart wide as infinity
Listened, and captured the inaudible
Cadences that awake the occult ear:
Out of the ineffable hush it hears them come
Trembling with the beauty of wordless speech,
And thoughts too great and deep to find a voice,
Thoughts whose desire new-makes the universe.
A scale of sense that climbed with fiery feet
To heights of unimagined happiness,

Recast his being's aura in joy-glow,
His body glimmered like a skyey shell;
His gates to the world were swept with seas of light.
Savitri: Book II, Canto 9, p. 267.

Commentary

The Occult Ear

The sphere of Bliss where Aswapathy arrives is the sphere of the soul's sharpened sensitivities. The ear listens to occult sounds. There wordless speech is the fullest sound. There mortal thought has an immortal voice. There the body is aglow with the aura of supreme delight. There all things are swept by the sea's surges of the Supramental Light.

DETAILED NOTES

198. *Scents and Wonder-Hues*

The subtle scents and colours of the other worlds.

199. *The Occult Ear*

The subtle clairaudience of the super-conscious fields of the Light.

200. *Being's Aura*

The shifting shades of the invisible subtle bodies of the spirit aglow with the Fire Divine.

201. *Seas of Light*

The immeasurable oceans of the supreme Ray which enfold all the fields of the rare substances.

29

THE DIRE DELIGHT

A dire delight shook Aswapathy's body.

In sudden moments of revealing flame,
In passionate responses half-unveiled

He reached the rim of ecstasies unknown;
A touch supreme surprised his hurrying heart,
The clasp was remembered of the Wonderful.
And hints leaped down of white beatitudes.
Eternity drew close disguised as Love
And laid its hand upon the body of Time.
A little gift comes from the Immensitudes,
But measureless to life its gain of joy;
All the untold Beyond is mirrored there.
A giant drop of the Bliss unknowable
Overwhelmed his limbs and round his soul became
A fiery ocean of felicity:
He foundered drowned in sweet and burning vasts:
The dire delight that could shatter mortal flesh,
The rapture that the gods sustain he bors.
Immortal pleasure cleaned him in its waves
And turned his strength into undying power.
Immortality captured Time and carried Life.

Savitri: Book II, Canto 9, pp. 268-269

Commentary

The Rim of Ecstasies

The Force of the Absolute in the whirlwinds of rapture seizes Aswapathy and carries him to the rim of the Ecstasies. The hymns of the white beatitudes, Eternity's self veiled as love, took hold of the king hurrying him through innumerable worlds of the Bliss. An immeasurable sea of Power sways his limbs. In the burning vasts his spirit falters and flounders. For the dread flash of the Light of God shatters these sheaths of the flesh. Then the undying Force breaks the bounds of Time and with a supramental touch transforms the mind of Aswapathy.

DETAILED NOTES

202. *The Rim of Ecstasies*

The field of Matter, Mind and Life is the first field created by the Supermind. Beyond these are the pure terrains of the Supermind. Beyond are the Supreme ranges of the Bliss. Beyond the Bliss is the rim of the Triune Ecstasies.

203. *The White Beatitudes*

The lower ranger of the fields of the Light.

204. *The Untold Beyond*

Reflections of the fields of the Absolute mirrored in the glass of the Supermind.

205. *Drop of the Bliss*

The rain of the Bliss.

206. *Ocean of Felicity*

The seas of the Bliss encompassing the soul.

207. *Burning Vast*

The dazzling light of the solitudes of God.

208. *The Dire Delight*

The force of the absolute Bliss.

30

THE CLOSE OF IGNORANCE

Aswapathy glimpsed the borders of the Intuitive Mind.

Thought dances hand in hand with Nescience
On the grey road that winds towards the Sun.
Even while her fingers fumble at the knots
Which bind them to their strange companionship,
Into the moments of their marriage strife
Sometimes break flashes of the enlightening Fire.
Even now great thoughts are here that walk alone:
Armed they have come with the infallible word
In an investiture of intuitive light
That is a sanction from the eyes of God;

Announcers of a distant Truth they flame
Arriving from the rim of eternity.
A fire shall come out of the infinitudes,
A greater Gnosis shall regard the world
Crossing out of some far omniscience
On lustrous seas from the still rapt Alone
To illumine the deep heart of self and things.
A timeless knowledge it shall bring to Mind.
Its aim to life, to Ignorance its close.

Savitri: Book II: Canto X, pp. 292-293

Commentary

The Fire of the Infinitudes

Aswapathy approaches the regions of the Intuitive Mind. Thought the child of nescience, with its little ray vainly seeks to break the knot of Matter, Mind and Life. The intuition descending from the rims of eternity brings the fire of the Infinitudes to illumine Matter. Within the body of the intuitive Mind are held in a larger promise rays of the Supermind which shall bring to a close the dim domains of Nescience.

DETAILED NOTES

209. *Nescience*

The field of the appearances in which thought searches for the Light of the Supermind.

210. *Road*

The evolution from Mind to Supermind.

211. *Knots*

The knots of body Life and Mind which are changed into Supermind.

212. *Intuitive Light*

The light of the Intuitive Mind below the ranges of the Supramental Being.

213. *Rim of Eternity*

DISTANT TRUTHS BROUGHT BY THE Intuitive Light from ranges of the Triune Ecstasies.

214. *A Greater Gnosis*

The supreme knowledge of the Supermind.

215. *Close*

The close of the fields of ignorance after their transmutation into Supermind.

31

THE LIFE THOUGHT

Aswapathy contacted the Pure Mind of the Cosmos.

A power to uplift the laggard world,
Imperious rode a huge high-winged Life-Thought
Unwont to tread the firm unchanging soil:
Accustomed to a blue infinity,
It planed in sunlit sky and starlit air;
It saw after the unreached Immortal's home
And heard after the voices of the gods.
Iconoclast and shatterer of Time's forts.
Overleaping limit and exceeding norm,
It lit the thoughts that glow through the centuries
And moved to acts of superhuman force.
As far as its self-winged airplanes could fly,
Visiting the future in great brilliant raids
It reconnoitried vistas of dream-fate.
Apt to conceive, unable to attain,
It drew its concept-maps and vision-plans
Too large for the architecture of mortal Space.
Beyond in wideness where no footing is,
An imagist of bodiless Ideas,
Impassive to the cry of life and sense,
A pure Thought-Mind surveyed the cosmic act.
Archangel of a white transcending realm,

It saw the world from solitary heights
Luminous in a remote and empty air.
Savitri: Book II, Canto 10, pp. 293-294.

Commentary

Bodiless Ideas

Above the welter of our thoughts are bodiless ideas. These wing their way from transcendental realms into the fields of concepts. These reconnoitre the domains of our dreams. These with point and compass draw the maps of Mind. From solitary heights the pure thought surveys the roads of Mind. Aswapathy thus reaches the plane of Archetypal Ideas.

DETAILED NOTES

216. *Life Thought*

For the occultist a thought is not an abstraction. Thought for the esoteric eye has concrete form.

217. *It Planed*

Here thought is seen in the imagery of an aeroplane descending into the field of the Mind.

218. *Vistas*

Vistas of the mental field.

219. *Concep-Maps*

The plans of the Life-thought for the working out of fate.

220. *Bodiless Ideas*

The Archetypal Plane where thought is born.

221. *Thought Mind*

The Mind of the pure conceptions which surveys the cosmic scene.

222. *It Saw*

The mental perception of the realms of transcendence.

32

IDEAL SPACE

Aswapathy entered the sanctuary of Ideal Space.

In its vast ambit of ideal Space
Where beauty and mightiness walk hand in hand,
The Spirit's truths take form as living Gods
And each can build a world in its own right.
In an air which doubt and error cannot mark
With the stigmata of their deformity,
In communion with the musing privacy
Of a truth that sees in an unerring light
Where the sight falters not nor wanders thought,
Exempt from our world's exorbitant tax of tears,
Dreaming its luminous creations gaze.
On the Ideas that people eternity.
In a sun-blaze of joy and absolute power
Above the Masters of the Ideal throne
In sessions of secure felicity,
In regions of illumined certitude.
Far are those realms from our labour and yearning and call
Perfection's reign and hallowed sanctuary
Closed to the uncertain thoughts of human mind.
Remote from the turbid tread of mortal life.

Savitri: Book II, Canto 11, pp. 296-97

Commentary

The Planes of the Ideal Mind

Aswapathy's Spirit visits the broad spaces of the ideal Mind where thought builds in form our world of body and Mind. In Ideal Space where perception totters not and where thought stumbles not, where no tear taints the lids of Time, the Masters of the Ideal Throne build in felicity the world of Matter and Mind.

DETAILED NOTES

223. *Ideal Space*

The amphitheatre of Space in which the Masters construct the realms of Matter.

224. *Ideal Throne*

The throne of Absolute Power where the Masters draw the concept plans of the world to be.

33

THE STAIRS OF THOUGHT

Aswapathy climbed the stairs of thought
which lead to the place of Eternity.

There runs in its flow honeying the bosom of Space
A laughter from the immortal heart of Bliss
And the unfathomed Joy of timelessness,
The sound of Wisdom's murmur in the Unknown
And the breath of an unseen Infinity.
In gleaming clarities of amethyst air
The chainless and omnipotent Spirit of Mind
Brooded on the blue lotus of the Idea.
A gold supernal sun of timeless Truth
Poured down the mystery of the eternal Ray
Through a silence quivering with the word of Light
On an endless ocean of discovery.
Far-off he saw the joining hemispheres.
On meditation's mounting edge of trance
Great stairs of thought climbed up to unborn heights
Where Time's last ridges touch eternity's skies
And Nature speaks to the spirit's absolute.

Savitri: Book II, Canto 11, pp. 299-300

Commentary

The Mounting Edge of Trance

On ascending the stairs of trance, the Spirit of Aswapathy climbs the spheres of thought. In the clarities of the Supramental air he comprehends the nature of the ideas which build the world of mind. To him all thought appears as a Lotus in the azure water which takes its nourishment through its roots in the lowest bed of slime, and thence springs to the surface with all its petals of lovely bloom, and there-after seeks the Light and air of the sun above; so thought embedded in the mud seeks its escape into the Super-conscious Light. Then Aswapathy exceeding the mortal range has intimate glimpse of the rays of the Supramental Sun. In dim distance he sees the Lower hemispheres of Matter, Mind and Life joined with the higher hemispheres of the Triune Ecstasies. Thence, Aswapathy soaring beyond the ridges of the Supermind alights on the field of the Absolute Ray.

DETAILED NOTES

225. *Clarities of the Amethyst Air*

The clarities of the Supramental vision.

226. *Blue Lotus*

The blue lotus is the symbol of mind seeking from the waters below the vastitude of the air of the Supermind above.

227. *Supernal Sun*

The orb of the Supramental Light.

228. *Joining Hemispheres*

The merging of the Lower Hemispheres of Body, Mind and Life with the Higher Hemispheres of the Triune Ecstasies.

229. *Great Stairs of Thought*

The stairs of the ascension from Mind into Supermind.

230. *Last Ridges*

The last ridges of the Supermind.

231. *The Spirit's Absolute*

The last ascension into the field of the Triune Ecstasies.

34

BEYOND THE TRIPLE STAIRS

Passing the lower stairs of Body, Mind and Life, the lower Trilogy of the Integral Yoga, Aswapathy stepped beyond the upper triple stairs—the higher Trilogy leading to Supermind and Sachchidananda.

In a sublimer and more daring soar
To the wide summit of the triple stairs
Bare steps climbed up like glowing rocks of gold
Burning their way to a pure absolute sky.
August and few the sovereign Kings of Thought
Have made of Space their wide all-seeing gaze
Surveying the enormous work of Time:
A Breadth of all-containing Consciousness
Supported being in a still embrace.
Intercessors with a luminous Unseen.
They captain the long passage to the world
The imperatives of the creator Self
Obeyed by unknowing earth, by conscious heaven;
Their thoughts are partners in its vast control.
A great all-ruling consciousness is there
And Mind unwitting serves a higher Power;
It is a channel, not the source of all.
The cosmos is no accident in Time;
There is a meaning in each play of Chance,
There is a freedom in each face of Fate.
A Wisdom knows and guides the mysteried world;
A truth-gaze shapes its beings and events;
A Word self-born upon creation's heights,
Voice of the Eternal in the temporal spheres,
Prophet of the seeings of the Absolute,
Sows the Idea's significance in Form
And from that seed the growths of Time arise.
On peaks beyond our ken the All Wisdom sits:
A single and infallible look comes down.
A silent touch from the supernal's air
Awakes to ignorant knowledge in its acts

The secret power in the inconscient depths.
Compelling the blinded Godhead to emerge,
Determining Necessity's rude dance
As she passes through the circuit of the hours
And vanishes from the chase of finite eyes
Down circling vistas of asonic Time.

Savitri: Book II, Canto 11, pp. 307-308

Commentary

The Secret Power

In a sublime soaring into the skies of the Absolute, Aswapathy rises step by unfaltering step from the lower stairs of Matter, Mind and Life to the higher stairs of the Triune Ecstasies. There he meets the sovereign few, the Adepts of the Supramental Light. There he merges with the all rolling consciousness of the Absolute Ray. There the lower mind appears as a mere channel of the Supreme Force serving the call of the higher power. There is no play of chance. Wisdom guides the movement of all beings and all events. Thence the voice of the Eternal scatters the seeds of ideas, shapened by its imperatives, into form of the fields of Time and Space. There the secret power in the inconscient depths by a subtle touch awakens the blind mind and blind matter into Light. When its work is done, the Ray vanishes from **the sight** of finite eyes back to the last vistas of the Light.

DETAILED NOTES

232. *The Triple Stairs*

The effulgent stairs of the Triune Ecstasies.

233. *Kings of Thought*

The Masters of the Supramental Light.

234. *Mind*

The lower channels of the Supramental Ray.

235. *Form*

The forms of the Supramental Light.

236. *The Secret Power*

The hidden force of the Supermind in the matrix of matter.

237. *Emerge*

The emergence of the Supermind from the veils of Body, Mind and Life.

238. *Vistas*

The vistas of the unhooded rays of the Supermind.

35

THE IDEAL MIND

The effulgent stair of the Ideal Mind was seen.

At either end of each effulgent stair
The heavens of the ideal Mind were seen
In a blue lucency of dreaming space
Like strips of brilliant sky clinging to the moon.
On one side glimmered hue on floating hue,
In a glory and surprise of the seized soul
And a tremulous rapture of the heart's insight
And the spontaneous bliss that beauty gives,
The lovely kingdoms of the deathless Rose.
Above the spirit cased in mortal sense
Are superconscious realms of heavenly peace,
Below, the Inconscient's sullen dim abyss,
Between, behind our life, the deathless Rose.

Savitri : Book II, Canto 12, pp. 314-315

Commentary

The Radiant Stairs of the Ascensions

From the lowest stair of the ascensions — the field of Matter and Mind — Aswapathy rises into the light of the Ideal Mind. Above are the higher ranges of the illumined mind, below is the abyss of Matter. In the middle region is the field of the Deathless Rose the symbol of the Supermind.

DETAILED NOTES

239. *Effulgent Stair*

At the extreme end of Matter, Mind and Life, the triple stairs of the Lower Trilogy and at the extreme edge of the higher Trilogy of the Triune Ecstasies, the radiant light of God reigns and rules.

240. *The Ideal Mind*

The summit of the Ideal Mind points to the wider ranges of the Supramental Light.

241. *Kingdoms of the Deathless Rose*

The kingdoms of the Supramental Light.

242. *Spirit Cased in Mortal Sense*

The soul imprisoned in Body, Mind and Life.

243. *The Inconscient's Sullen Dim Abyss*

The last Abyss of Matter.

36

THE DISCLOSURE

Aswapathy arrived at the final plane of Bliss.

Then by a touch, a presence or a voice
The world is turned into a temple ground
And all discloses the unknown Beloved.
In an outburst of heavenly joy and ease
Life yields to the divinity within
And gives the rapture-offering of its all,
And the soul opens to felicity.
A bliss is felt that never can wholly cease,
A sudden mystery of secret Grace
Flowers goldening our earth of red desire.
All the high gods who hid their visages
From the soiled passionate ritual of our hopes
Reveal their names and their undying powers.

A fiery stillness wakes the slumbering cells,
A passion of the flesh becoming spirit,
And marvellously is fulfilled at last
The miracle for which our life was made.

Savitri : Book II, Canto 12, pp. 315-316

Commentary

The Unveiling of Divinity

At the touch of the Presence, the falling veils of the divine disclose to Aswapathy the grandeur and the grace of God. The submerged Divinity, lost in matter's depths is discovered touched and known.

DETAILED NOTES

244. *Touch*
The Supramental awakening of the Spirit.

245. *Secret Grace*
The concealed Supermind.

246. *The Miracle*
The miracle of the triple transformation of Body, Mind and Life into the Supermind.

37

THE EPIPHANY

Aswapathy climbed through invisible worlds of colour and ecstasy.

Here upon earth are early awakenings,
Moments that tremble in an air divine,
And grown upon the yearning of her soil
Time's sun-flowers' gaze at gold Eternity :
There are the imperishable beatitudes.
A million lotuses swaying on one stem,
World after coloured and ecstatic world
Climbs towards some far unseen epiphany.

Savitri : Book II, Canto 12, pp-316-317

Commentary

The Supramental Manifestation

From the early awakenings, from the subtle transformation of Body, Mind and Life emerges for Aswapathy the full radiance of the Supramental manifestation. The ambit of his gaze now enfolds the invisible worlds of the beatitudes. As sunflowers pend from a single stalk, as a million lotuses droop from one stem, so all the worlds of the ascending substances stoop from the single Ray of the Supermind.

DETAILED NOTES

247. *Early Awakening*

The primal transformation psychic, spiritual and supramental of man which leads to the realisation of the Absolute Light.

248. *Imperishable Beatitudes*

The worlds of the Bliss.

249. *The Unseen Epiphany*

The Supramental manifestation.

38

THE AGELESS RAY

On the heights lay the Supreme Truth —
the Ageless Ray of the Absolute Spirit.

A fire along the mystic paths of earth,
It rises through the mortal's hemisphere,
Till borne by runners of the Day and Dusk
It enters the occult eternal Light
And clambers whitening to the invisible Throne.
Its worlds are steps of an ascending Force :
A dream of giant contours, titan lines,
Homes of unfallen and illumined Might,

Heavens of unchanging Good pure and unborn,
Heights of the grandeur of Truth's ageless ray,
As in a symbol sky they start to view
And call our souls into a vaster air.
On their summits they bear up the sleepless Flame;
Dreaming of a mysterious Beyond,
Transcendent of the paths of Fate and Time,
They point above themselves with index peaks
Through a pale-sapphire ether of God-mind
Towards some gold Infinite's apocalypse.
A thunder rolling mid the hills of God,
Tireless, severe is their tremendous Voice :
Exceeding us, to exceed ourselves they call
And bid us rise incessantly above.

Savitri : Book II, Canto 12, pp-317-318

Commentary

Infinite's Apocalypse

From the mystic paths of Matter and Mind, from the air of the Lower hemisphere, the Spirit of Aswapathy enters the Ring of the Occult Light. Rarer and ever rarer it ascends to the throne of the Invisible. At the last edge of the Light, it touches the truth of the Ageless Ray. Transcendent of the robes of Fate and Time, in unceasing ascensions through rarer worlds of ever rarer hues, exceeding all thoughts and all dreams, the soul of Aswapathy merges into the Infinite.

DETAILED NOTES

250. *Mystic Paths of Earth*

The varied roads of all the evolutions out of Earth to Supermind.

251. *Mortal's Hemisphere*

The Lower Trilogy of Matter, Mind and Life.

252. *Invisible Throne*

The throne of the Divine Light.

253. *Ageless Ray*
The uncreated Ray of the Absolute.

254. *Infinite's Apocalypse*
The last rending of the veils reveals the Supermind.

39

THE SURRENDER

Book II closes with Aswapathy's total surrender to the Supreme Force of the Mother before which he falls prone in unconscious trance.

Then in a sovereign answer to his heart
A gesture came as of worlds thrown away,
And from her raiment's lustrous mystery raised
One arm half-parted the eternal veil.
A light appeared still and imperishable.
Attracted to the large and luminous depths
Off the ravishing enigma of her eyes,
He saw the mystic outline of a face.
Overwhelmed by her implacable light and bliss,
An atom of her illimitable self
Mastered by the honey and lightning of her power,
Tossed towards the shores of her ocean ecstasy,
Drunk with a deep golden spiritual wine,
He cast from the rent stillness of his soul
A cry of adoration and desire
And the surrender of his boundless mind
And the self-giving of his silent heart.
He fell down at her feet unconscious, prone.

Savitri : Book II, Canto 14, pp. 334-335

Commentary

The Sovereign Gesture

By a sovereign gesture the Absolute Radiance rends the raiment of matter and by a rare raising of the veil reveals the Face of the Divine. The enigma of earthly eyes it dissolves. Inebriate with the honey of the wine of Bliss, with a cry of adoration and desire, yielding his heart and mind to the Light Aswapathy falls unconscious at the feet of the Ray.

DETAILED NOTES

255. *Gesture*

The gesture of the Supramental Light revealing the Face of the Ray.

256. *Raiment*

The covering of Body, Mind and Life hiding the Supramental Light.

257. *The Face*

The face of the Absolute Light.

258. *Spiritual Wine*

The flow and flood of the Absolute Delight in the veins of Aswapathy.

259. *Surrender*

The last surrender of Aswapathy in answer to the gesture of the Light.

260. *Unconscious*

The body, Mind and Life of Aswapathy fall into unconsciousness under the pressure of the Ray.

40

THE MYSTIC PEAKS

Knowledge called Aswapathy to the mystic peaks of the Truth.

Out of the neutral silence of his soul
He passed to its fields of puissance and of calm
And saw the Powers that stand above the world,
Traversed the realms of the supreme Idea
And sought the summit of created things
And the almighty source of cosmic change.

There knowledge called him to her mystic peaks
Where thought is held in a vast internal sense
And feeling swims across a sea of peace
And vision climbs beyond the reach of Time.
An equal of the first creator seers,
Accompanied by an all-revealing light
He moved through regions of transcendent Truth
Inward, immense, innumerably one.
There distance was his own huge spirit's extent;
Delivered from the fictions of the mind
Mind's triple dividing step baffled no more;
Its inevitable and continuous streams,
The long flow of its manifesting course,
Was held in spirit's single wide regard.

Savitri : Book II, Canto 15, p. 338

Commentary

Deliverance from Mind

Stepping forth from the triple stairs of Body, Mind and Life and passing out of the neutral zone and silences of the soul, Aswapathy from the realms of the Supreme Idea seeks the summit of created things where-in are wrought all cosmic changes. Upon his closed lids is the call of the mystic peaks of the higher mind and the soaring ranges of the Intuitive Light. The King moves into the regions of transcendent truth where the great creators the Masters of the Light build all the worlds from Supermind to Mind. In his merging with the One, he is delivered from the illusions of the mind. In the spirit's single regard Aswapathy beholds the entire epiphany of the Absolute.

DETAILED NOTES

261. *Neutral Silence*

The neutral zones that divide the worlds rare and gross of all the regions of the Absolute Ray.

262. *Powers*

The masters of the Ray.

263. *Supreme Idea*
Mental approach to the Supermind.

264. *Source of Cosmic Change*
The regions of the Supermind whence all creation springs.

265. *Mystic Peaks*
The mystic peaks of Intuitive Mind and Mind of Light pointing to the heights of the Supermind.

266. *Regions of Transcendent Truth*
The regions of the Supreme Truth, Supermind.

267. *Delivered*
The deliverance from the illusions of the Mind by the liberating Light of Supermind.

268. *Mind's Triple Dividing Step*
The triple stairs of Body, Mind and Life moving to the Triune Ecstasies.

41

THE RIM OF THE UNKNOWABLE

BEYOND THE TRIPLE Heaven at the extreme horizon of the Spirit Aswapathy beheld the Rim of the unknowable.

His sight surpassed creation's head and base;
Ablaze the triple heavens revealed their suns,
The obscure abyss exposed its monstrous rule.
All but the ultimate Mystery was his field,
Almost the Unkowable disclosed its rim.
His self's infinities began to emerge,
The hidden universes cried to him;
Eternities called to eternities
Sending their speechless message still remote.
Arisen from the marvel of the depths
And burning from the superconscious height

And sweeping in great horizontal gyres
A million energies joined and were the One
All flowed immeasurably to one sea:
All living forms became its atom homes.
A Pan-energy that harmonised all life
Held now existence in its vast control;
A portion of that majesty he was made.
At will he lived in the unoblivious Ray.

Savitri: Book II, Canto 15, p. 340

Commentary

The Pan-Energy

The Pan-energy of the Supramental Force, as a magnet, draws Aswapathy to the regions of the Unoblivious Ray. Passing from the Abyss of Matter, rising to the head and source of created things Supermind Aswapathy moves into the realms of the Triune Ecstasies. On the rim of the unknowable is the rule of night.

All the divided energies leave their division and are gathered into the Pan-energy of the One. Absorbed into Supermind Aswapathy's soul becomes one with the Cosmic Whole.

DETAILED NOTES

269. *Creation's Head and Base*

The base of creation is the last abyss of matter; the head of creation is the region of the Supermind.

270. *Triple Heavens*

The triple heavens of the Triune Ecstasies.

271. *The Obscure Abyss*

The abyss of Matter.

272. *The Ultimate Mystery*

The ultimate mystery of the Triune Ecstasies.

273. *The One*

The Absolute wherein all energies meet.

274. *A Pan-Energy*

The Universal Cosmic Force.

275. *The Unoblivious Ray*

The Supermind.

42

THE NOUGHT

Rising out of the plane of Mind, Luminous, Intuitive and Overmind, Aswapathy in Book III, the Book of the Divine Mother, reaches the plane of Supermind. He enters the region of impalpable Nought.

Only a formless Form of self was left,
A tenuous ghost of something that had been,
The last experience of a lapsing wave
Before it sinks into a bourneless sea,
As if it kept even on the brink of Nought
Its bare feeling of the ocean whence it came.
A vastness brooded free from sense of Space,
An Everlastingness out off from Time;
A strange sublime unalterable Peace
Silent rejected from it world and soul.
A stark companionless Reality
Answered at last to his soul's passionate search:
Passionless, wordless, absorbed in its fathomless hush,
Keeping the mystery none would ever pierce,
It brooded inscrutable and intangible
Facing him with its dumb tremendous calm.

Savitri: Book III, Canto 1, pp. 348-349

Commentary

The Companionless Reality

Ascending from the Formless Form of Self in the last experience of the lapsing wave, the Spirit of Aswapathy faces the companionless Reality of the Absolute.

DETAILED NOTES

276. *Formless Form of Self*

The bodies of the self in subtle form which are shed when Aswapathy passes into the regions of the Absolute Ray.

277. *The Last Experience*

The Spirit's passing from the fields of the Supermind into the planes of the Triune Ecstasies.

278. *Brink of Nought*

Nothingness is the symbol of invisibility. The brink is a crucial point from one zone of life to another. It is nothing to the lower mind. It is substance to the rarer perceptions of the Supermind.

279. *Companionless Reality*

The field of the Absolute.

43

THE BARE INFINITE

Aswapathy beheld the bare Infinite.

A pure existence safe from thought and mood,
A consciousness of unshared immortal bliss,
It dwelt aloof in its bare infinite,
One and unique, unutterably sole,
A Being formless, featureless and mute,
That knew itself by its own timeless self,
Aware for ever in its motionless depths,
Uncreating, uncreated, and unborn,
The One by whom all live, who lives by none,
An immeasurable luminous secrecy
Guarded by the veils of the Unmanifest,
Above the changing cosmic interlude
Abode supreme, immutably the same,

A silent Cause occult, impenetrable,
Infinite, eternal, unthinkable, alone.

Savitri: Book III , Canto 1, pp. 349-350

Commentary

The Uncreated Light

Aswapathy's Spirit ascends into the field of the Pure Existence. Robbed of all the relativities and conditions of the lower life, the King faces the bare Ray of the Unmanifest. The Absolute Spirit, without form or feature, beyond Time and Space, Alone Uncreated and Unborn, in immeasurable Light and unutterable secrecy, the occult cause of things, now appears shorn of all attributes as the One that holds all created life in an unique unity.

DETAILED NOTES

280. *The Bare Infinite*

The Absolute—free of all limitations and conditions.

281. *One*

The Absolute and the Alone.

282. *A Being*

The Absolute without attributes, the immutable Brahma of the Bhagavadgita.

283. *Uncreated and Unborn*

The Absolute is free of the conditions of birth of creation or life or death.

284. *The Veils*

The veils of Body, Mind and Life.

285. *A Silent Cause*

The occult Absolute.

44

THE ORIGINAL BLISS

Aswapathy felt the coming of a Being of wisdom, the Infinite and Absolute.

Across the silence of the ultimate Calm,
Out of a marvellous Transcendence' core,
A body of wonder and translucency
As if a sweet mystic summary of her self
Escaping into the original Bliss
Had come enlarged out of eternity,
Someone came infinite and Absolute.
A being of wisdom, power and delight,
Even as a mother draws her child to her arms,
Took to her breast Nature and world and soul.
Abolishing the signless emptiness,
Breaking the vacancy and voiceless hush
Piercing the limitless Unknowable,
Into the liberty of the motionless depths
A beautiful and felicitous lustre stole,
Imaged itself in a surprising beam
And built a golden passage to his heart
Touching through him all longing sentient things.

Savitri: Book III, Canto 2, p. 353-354

Commentary

The Embodied Beam

From the ultimate calm, out of the heart of subtle transcendences, the Formless Ray takes a form. A body of wonder, a body of Bliss, a body of wisdom draws, as a mother draws to the infant, to the corporeal essences of the Spirit of Aswapathy. With one flash of its light it destroys the signless vacancy of matter. From motionless depths the lustrous sheen passes through subtle channels into the heart of Aswapathy.

DETAILED NOTES

286. *A body of Wonder*
The embodied Light.

287. *Original Bliss*
The real substance of the Bodiless Ray.

288. *A Being of Wisdom*
God incarnate in wisdom.

289. *Breaking the Vacancy*
Shattering the apparent emptiness of matter.

290. *A Surprising Beam*
The unembodied Ray.

291. *A Golden Passage*
The subtle channels of the force rushing to the heart of Aswapathy.

45

THE TRACTS OF LIGHT

Aswapathy passed the tracts of invisible superconscient Light and reached the sempiternal base of life.

As one who sets his sail towards mysteried shores
Driven through huge oceans by the breath of God,
The fathomless below, the unknown around,
His soul abandoned the blind star-field, Space.
After from all that makes the measured world,
Plunging to hidden eternities it withdrew
Back from mind's foaming surface to the Vasts
Voiceless within us in omniscient sleep.
Above the imperfect reach of word and thought,
Beyond the sight, the last support of form,
Lost in deep tracts of superconscient Light,
Or voyaging in blank featureless nothingness,

Sole in the trackless Incommensurable,
Or past not-self and self and selflessness,
Transgressing the dream-shores of conscious mind
He reached at last his sempiternal base.
On sorrowless heights no winging cry disturbs,
Pure and untouched above the mortal play
Is spread the spirit's hushed immobile air.

Savitri: Book III, Canto 3, p. 363

Commentary

The Immobile Air

From the blind star-field of matter, out of the domain of measured Space, plunging into the field of all the worlds of the eternities, pushing beyond the sights of the human lid, pressing beyond the support of forms, voyaging through the tracts of the superconscient Light, sailing through the immensities of the apparent vacancies of matter, Aswapathy arrives at the sempiternal base of the Triune Ecstasies; breathings the rare air of the Immobile Ray.

DETAILED NOTES

292. *Blind Star-Field*

The worlds of Matter and Mind.

293. *Measured World*

The rings of the material fields bounded by Matter and Mind.

294. *Hidden Eternities*

The fields of subtle matter.

295. *Foaming Surface*

The surface fields of Mind.

296. *Tracts of Superconscient Light*

The deeper worlds of the Supramental Ray beyond Matter and Mind.

297. *Featureless Nothingness*
The invisible fields of the immutable.

298. *Not Self*
The Self of Body, Mind and Matter.

299. *Self*
The individual soul or Jiva.

300. *Selflessness*
The Universal Soul or Atma.

301. *Sempiternel Base*
The base of the Triune Ecstasies.

302. *Immobile Air*
The subtle air of the Supermind.

46

TRUTH'S GIANT BASE

At Truth's giant base, at the source of things, stand the guardians of Eternity.

Armed with the immune occult unsinking Fire
The guardians of Eternity keep its law
For ever fixed upon Truth's giant base
In her magnificent and termless home.
There Nature on her dumb spiritual couch
Immutably transcendent knows her source
And to the stir of multitudinous worlds
Assents unmoved in a perpetual calm.
All-causing, all-sustaining and aloof,
The Witness looks from his unshaken poise.
An Eye immense regarding all things done.

Savitri: Book III, Canto 3, p. 364

Commentary

The Eye of God

The Eye of God looks with unperturbed regard upon the worlds above and the realms below. It sees fixed in truth the Masters of the Light who move the stars and the suns in immutable calm.

DETAILED NOTES

303. *Guardians of Eternity*

Masters of the Light.

304. *Truth's Giant Base*

The base of the Supreme truth of the Triune Ecstasies.

305. *Witness*

The cosmic gaze in unimperturbable poise.

306. *An Eye Immense*

The Eyes of the Divine.

47

THE GAZE OF THE DIVINE MOTHER

Aswapathy met at last the gaze of the Eternal Matter fixed upon his ascending movement.

The One he worshipped was within him now:
Flame-pure, ethereal—tressed almighty Face
Appeared and lips moved by immortal words;
Lids, wisdom's leaves, drooped over rapture's orbs.
A marble monument of ponderings, shone
A forehead, sight's crypt, and large like ocean's gaze
Towards Heaven two tranquil eyes of boundless thought
Looked into man's and saw the god to come.

Savitri: Book III, Canto 4, p. 379

Commentary

The Eye of the Boundless

The One moulded into form, the Face Divine with lips of immortal speech, with lids of rapture drooping with wisdom's glances; a brow of calm, an eye of boundless thoughts wide as the ocean's surge marks in Aswapathy the emergence of the concealed Light of the Supermind from the coverings of matter.

DETAILED NOTES

307. *The One*
The Absolute.

308. *Almighty Face*
The Face of the embodied Absolute.

309. *Ocean's Gaze*
The Cosmic Gaze.

310. *Eyes of Boundless Thought*
The eye of the cosmic perception.

48

THE INVOCATION OF ASWAPATHY

Aswapathy invoked the Eternal Mother to mission to Earth her living Form, the embodiment of knowledge, Love and Beauty, to unlock the doors of Fate and to transform the human Race.

O radiant fountain of the world's delight
World-free and unattainable above.
O Bliss who ever dwellst deep hid within
While men seek thee outside and never find,
Mystery and Muse with hieratic tongue,
Incarnate the white passion of thy force,
Mission to earth some living form of thee.
One moment fill with thy eternity,
Let thy infinity in one body live.

All-Knowledge wrap one mind in seas of light.
All-love throb single in one human heart,
Immortal, treading the earth with mortal feet
All heaven's beauty crowd in earthly limbs:
Omnipotence, girdle with the power of God.
Movements and moments of a mortal will,
Pack with the eternal might one human hour
And with one gesture change all future time.
Let a great word be spoken from the heights
And one great act unlock the doors of Fate.

Savitri: Book III, Canto 4, pp. 390-391

Commentary

Aswapathy's Prayer for the Descent of Supermind in the form of Savitri

While the errant mind of man vainly seeks the Divine in the fields of appearances, Aswapathy's spirit in a deeper musing invokes the radiant Light in a human form to descend into the heart of matter, to unlock the doors of fate, and to subdue the yoke of the God of Death. With hieratic tongue Aswapathy conjures the birth of the white passion of the Force. His is the ardent call for the incarnation of Savitri. Savitri is the finite infinite—a form embodying the Absolute presence, Savitri is the symbol of the Supramental Light veiled in matter. Hers is the heaven-sent mission to open the chamber of fate. Hers is the challenge to overthrow the first enemy of Life, Death.

DETAILED NOTES

311. *O Bliss*

The world of external matter which yields no fruit of knowledge to the seeker.

311. *Deep hid within*

The Absolute Delight hidden in Matter.

312. *Outside*

The world of external matter which yields no fruit of knowledge to the seeker.

313. *Mission to Earth*

The mission of Savitri in mortal form to unfasten the locks of fate and to defend the hostile force of Death.

314. *Infinity in One Body*

The Supramental Light hidden in the body of Savitri.

315. *Seas of Light*

The seas of the Supramental Light concealed in the mind of Savitri.

316. *The Human Hour*

The human hour of Savitri covering the Timeless moment of the sealed eternities of the Supramental Light.

317. *Doors of Fate*

The doors of Death shattered by the illumined Light of embodied Savitri.

49

INCARNATION OF SAVITRI

The Absolute answering the prayer, promised the Incarnation of Savitri to break the Iron Law of Material Nature.

O strong forerunner, I have heard thy cry.
One shall descend and break the iron Law,
Change Nature's doom by the lone Spirit's power.
A limitless Mind that can contain the world,
A sweet and violent heart of ardent calms
Moved by the passions of the gods shall come.
All mights and greatnesses shall join in her;
Beauty shall walk celestial on the earth,
Delight shall sleep in the cloud-net of her hair
And in her body as on his homing tree
Immortal Love shall beat his glorious wings.
A music of griefless things shall weave her charm;

The harps of the Perfect shall attune her voice.
The streams of Heaven shall murmur in her laugh,
Her lips shall be the honey-combs of God,
Her limbs his golden jars of ecstasy,
Her breasts the rapture-flowers of Paradise.
She shall bear Wisdom in her voiceless bosom,
Strength shall be with her like a conqueror's sword
And from her eyes the Eternal's bliss shall gaze.
A seed shall be sown in Death's tremendous hour,
A branch of heaven transplant to human soil;
Nature shall overleap her mortal step;
Fate shall be changed by an unchanging will.

Savitri: Book III, Canto 4, pp. 391-392

Commentary

The Descending Ray of Savitri

In answer to the cry of Aswapathy Savitri descends into the inconscient depths of Matter to break the bonds of Death. Within her body beats the music of the Supramental Ray in limitless perfection. Beauty informs her steps on earth. Delight murmurs about her aureate hair. Love lingers in the motion of her eyes. A silent charm plays upon her griefless lips scented with the honey of the Bliss of God. Her subtle body is a jar of ecstatic delight. A Supernal wisdom dwells in the hush of her lips. She is strength and Power. She is the sword unsheathed of the Supramental Light in readiness to slay the Dragon of Death.

DETAILED NOTES

318. *Cry*

The cry of Aswapathy for the conquering Light of the Divine.

319. *Iron Law*

The iron law of matter.

320. *Delight*

The Bliss of the Absolute Ray asleep in body's charm.

321. *Jars of Ecstasy*

All the subtle bodies which circumscribe the soul are as void jars spinning on the ecstasies of the Bliss.

322. *A Conqueror's Sword*

The sword of the Supermind.

323. *Overleap*

Transcendence of Death.

50

THE SUPRAMENTAL RACE A VISION

Aswapathy saw in the future the coming of the Supramental race.

I saw the Omnipotent's flaming pioneers
Over the heavenly verge which turns towards life
Come crowding down the amber stairs of birth;
Forerunners of a divine multitude
Out of the paths of the morning star they came
Into the little room of mortal life.
I saw them cross the twilight of an age,
The sun-eyed children of a marvellous dawn,
The great creators with wide brows of calm,
The massive barrier-breakers of the world
And wrestlers with destiny in her lists of will,
The labourers in the quarries of the gods,
The messengers of the Incommunicable,
The architects of immortality.
Into the fallen human sphere they came,
Faces that wore the Immortal's glory still,
Voice that communed still with the thoughts of God,
Bodies made beautiful by the Spirit's light,
Carrying the magic word, the mystic fire,
Carrying the Dionysian cup of joy,
Approaching eyes of a diviner man,
Lips chanting an unknown anthem of the soul

Feet echoing in the corridors of Time.

High priests of wisdom, sweetness, might and bliss,
Discoverers of beauty's sunlit ways
And swimmers of Love's laughing fiery floods
And dancers within rapture's golden doors,
Their tread one day shall change the suffering earth
And justify the light on Nature's face.

Savitri: Book III, Canto 4, p. 339

Commentary

The Supramental Descent of the Masters of the Light into Earth.

With the fall of the light of God into matter follows the incarnation of the adepts of the Light into the field of substance. From distant planetary schemes, from the morning stars of other worlds of life, they come by the stairs of birth into the little room of the material life. These flaming pioneers, these barrier-breakers of the world, come to the darkness of our fallen sphere bearing the magic word of the Mystic Ray and carrying the cup of Bliss. Their tread shall transform the suffering earth and Justify the ways of God and Man.

DETAILED NOTES

324. *Flaming Pioneers*

The Adepts of the Supramental Light.

325. *Paths of the Morning Star*

The distant planets of the rare worlds whence the Masters descend into matter.

326. *Little Room*

The field of Body, Mind and Life.

327. *Fallen Human Sphere*

The field of Matter.

328. *The Mystic Fire*

The Supramental Light.

The selections one to forty-eight of this book deal with the ascending yoga of Aswapathy, Selections forty-nine to the end are concerned with the descending yoga of Savitri. The ascending aspiration of Aswapathy and the descendiug ray of Savitri are the twin movements of the Integral Yoga which are necessary to complete the transformation of Body, Mind and Life into Supermind.

329. *Change*

The Supramental Transformation.

51

THE RETURN FROM TRANCE

Book III closes with the return from trance of Aswapathy. Here ends his Yoga of ascent.

Lone, brilliant, vacant lay the inner fields;
All was unfilled inordinate spirit space,
Indifferent, waste, a desert of bright peace.
Then a line moved on the far edge of calm:
The warm-lipped sentient soft terrestrial wave,
A quick and many-murmured moan and laugh,
Came gliding in upon white feet of sound.
Unlocked was the deep glory of Silence' heart;
The absolute unmoving stillnesses
Surrendered to the breath of mortal air,
Dissolving boundlessly the heavens of trance
Collapsed to waking mind. Eternity
Cast down its incommunicable lids
Over its solitudes remote from ken
Behind the voiceless mystery of sleep.

Savitri: Book II, Canto 4, pp. 392-393

Commentary

The Dissolution of Aswapathy's Trance

The inner fields of light, the absolute stillnesses, the heavens of the Supramental trance, dissolve as Aswapathy returns to the fields of matter.

DETAILED NOTES

330. *Inner Fields*

The rare worlds of substance withdrawn from Aswapathy's eyes by the closure of the Supramental trance.

331. *Terrestrial Wave*

The wave particles of gross matter calling back Aswapathy into the fields of Body, Mind and Life.

332. *Dissolving*

The dissolution of the Supramental trance.

52

THE CYCLE OF THE SEASONS

Book IV and the remaining books of the poem tell of the birth, the quest, the love, the marriage, the fate and the Yoga of descent of Savitri. The cycle of the Seasons preceding the birth of Savitri is described.

Across the burning langour of the soil
Paced Summer with his pomp of violent noons
And stamped his tyranny of torrid light
And the blue seal of a great burnished sky.
Next through its fiery swoon or clotted knot
Rain-tide burst in upon torn wings of heat,
Startled with lightnings air's unquiet drowse,
Lashed with life-giving streams the torpid soil,
Overcast with flare and sound and storm-winged dark
The star-defended doors of heaven's dim sleep,
Or from the gold eye of her paramour
Covered with packed cloud-veils the earth's brown face.
Armies of revolution crossed the time-field,
The cloud's unending march besieged the world,
Tempest's pronunciamentos claimed the sky
And thunder drums announced the embattled gods,
A traveller from unquiet neighbouring seas
The dense-maned monsoon rode neighing through earth's hours:
Thick now the emissary javelins:
Enormous lightnings split the horizon's rim
And, hurled from the quarters as from contending camps,

Married heaven's edges steep and bare and blind:
A surge and hiss and onset of huge rain,
The long straight sleet-drift, clamours of winged storm-charge,
Throngs of wind-faces, rushing of wind-feet
Hurrying swept through the prone afflicted plains:
Heaven's waters trailed and dribbled through the drowned land
Then all was a swift stride, a sibilant race,
Or all was tempest's shout and water's fall,
A dimness sagged on the grey floor or day,
Its dingy sprawling length joined morn to eve;
Wallowing in sludge and shower it reached black dark.
Savitri: Book IV, Canto 1, pp. 397-398

Commentary

The Yoga of Savitri

In the yoga of Savitri first is a fall into matter. The languor of the summer air, the break of the raintide from the lower heaven clouds, clamour of the sky, the din of the tempest and the howl of the water's fall are the signs of Savitri's yoga of the earth in her quest to touch the earth for earth's transmutation. She seeks the conquest of the dark and not a repose in the Light. It is by the reversal of the consciousness of earth that she strives for the transmutation of Body into the life Divine.

DETAILED NOTES

333. *Summer*

The symbol of the violent noons of matter.

334. *Clotted Knot*

The clotted knot of Matter, Mind and Life.

335. *Rain-Tide*

The symbol of the flood-tides of the Earth.

336. *Black Dark*

The field of matter which Savitri is pledged to destroy.

53

SAVITRI

Her name ran murmuring on the lips of men
Exalted and sweet like an inspired verse
Struck from the epic lyre of rumour's winds
Or sung like a chanted thought by the poet Fame.
But like a sacred symbol's was that cult.
Admired, unsought, intangible to the grasp
Her beauty and flaming strength were seen after
Like lightning playing with the fallen day,
A glory unapproachably divine.
No equal heart came close to join her heart,
No transient earthly love assailed her calm,
No hero passion had the strength to seize;
No eyes demanded her replying eyes.
A power within her awed the imperfect flesh;
The self-protecting genius in our clay
Divined the goddess in the woman's shape
And drew back from a touch beyond its kind,
The earth-nature bound in the sense-life's narrow made.

Savitri: Book IV, Canto 2, pp. 417-418

Commentary

The Divine Goddess in the Woman's Shape

The Ray which dwelt in her body ran in radiancy to the lips of men. But no heart aspires for her hand. No earthly love assaults her calm. No eyes seek her eyes. The very power within her awes the approach of the human touch.

DETAILED NOTES

337. *Murmuring on the Lips of Men*
The radiant Light of Savitri as a rare current runs on the lips of men.

338. *No Eyes*
All eyes are held back baffled by the Supramental Light.

339. *The Earth-Nature*

The earth-nature does not bind Savitri. On the contrary the super nature destroys the earth-nature. Savitri is the veiled destroyer of Matter, Mind and Life. Born in the women's shape she is liberate of the body; for she is the Supramental Light itself.

54

THE CALL OF SAVITRI

O rubies of silence, lips from which there stole
Low laughter, music of tranquillity,
Star-lustrous eyes awake in sweet large night
And limbs like fine-linked poems made of gold,
Stanzaed to glimmering curves by artist gods,
Depart where love and destiny call your charm.
Venture through the deep world to find thy mate.
For somewhere on the longing breast of earth,
Thy unknown lover waits for thee the unknown.

Savitri: Book IV, Canto 3, p. 425

Commentary

Love's Summon to Savitri

The ruby lips of love carved by the chisel of the Gods its lustrous eyes and its limbs of gold, summon by their charm Savitri to meet her destiny's call. The unknown lover Satyavan waits for the unknown love—Savitri in a silence.

DETAILED NOTES

340. *Rubies of Silence*

In the occult world speech is not expressed in words. The esoteric communication from soul to soul is in colour. The rose is the hue of love.

341. *Destiny*

For Savitri the call of love is a challenge to break the fetters of Death.

342. *Venture*

The venture of consciousness to meet the challenge of Death.

343. *Thy unknown Lover*

Satyavan.

344. *For the unknown*

Savitri unknown to Satyavan.

55

SAVITRI'S QUEST

Here timeless musings large and glad and still,
Men had forborne as yet to fill with cares,
Imperial acres of the eternal sowers
And wind-stirred grass-lands winking in the sun:
In the grove's murmurous bee-air humming wild
Or past the long lapsing voice of silver floods
Like a swift hope journeying among its dreams
Hastened the chariot of the golden bride.

Savitri: Book IV, Canto 4, p· 431

Commentary

The Chariot of the Bride

Through groves where the bee murmurs, in the wilds past lisping streams, Savitri's hastening dreams hurry to the arms of Satyavan.

DETAILED NOTES

335. *Grass-Lands*

Savitri makes no ascensions to fields above matter. Her chariot rolls through the grass-lands of earth. It is an earthly lover that she seeks. Her eyes are fixed to transform the earth into heaven. For her earth is heaven and heaven is earth. Savitri is the bridge between the Mind below and the Supermind above.

346. *The Chariot*

The chariot of Savitri passes through fields of Matter and not through world of the rare substances.

347. *The Golden Bride*

The aureate light of Supermind within the eyes of the bride of earth.

56

THE DESTINED MEETING PLACE

The spot where Savitri meets Satyavan was predestined.

But now the destined spot and hour were close;
Unknowing she had neared her nameless goal.
For though a dress of blind and devious chance
Is laid upon the work of all-wise Fate,
Our acts interpret an omniscient Force
That dwells in the compelling stuff of things,
And nothing happens in the cosmic play
But at its time and in its foreseen place.
To a space she came of soft and delicate air
That seemed a sanctuary of youth and joy,
A highland world of free and green delight
Where spring and summer lay together and strove
In indolent and amicable debate,
Inarmed, disputing with laughter who should rule.
There expectation beat wide sudden wings,
As if a soul had looked out from earth's face
And all that was in her felt a coming change
And forgetting obvious joys and common dreams,
Obedient to Time's call and the spirit's fate,

Were lifted to a beauty calm and pure
That lived under the eyes of Eternity.

Savitri: Book IV, Canto 1, p. 441

Commentary

The Appointed Hour and Spot of Love

No blind force of ignorant matter, no devious accident of Time drives Savitri into the embrace of Satyavan. The Omniscient Light, dwelling in nescient matter, guides the feet of Savitri to the foreseen spot the sanctuary of the forest where Satyavan dreams the dreams of God. At the appointed hour and spot the unknown lovers meet. The two eternities of two spirits indissolubly linked by fate join hands in matter's high delight.

DETAILED NOTES

348. *The Destined Spot*
The Ashram of Satyavan.

349. *All-Wise Fate*
The Omniscient force of the All-wise Fate and not chance fixed the meeting place of Satyavan and Savitri.

350. *The Cosmic Play*
The play of love in the heart of matter.

351. *Sanctuary*
The sanctuary of earth and not heaven.

352. *Green Delight*
The verdant delight of earth and not the spiritual delight of the Triune Ecstasies.

353. *A Coming Change*
The transmutation of earth into heaven wrought by the terrestrial kiss.

354. *Under the Eyes of Eternity*
But the earthly caress is deeply watched by the eyes of the Supermind above.

57

THE MEETING OF SAVITRI AND SATYAVAN

Gaze met close gaze and clung in sight's embrace.
A visage was there, noble and great and calm,
As if encircled by a halo of thought,
A span, an arc of meditating light,
As though some secret nimbus half was seen;
Her inner vision still remembering know
A forehead that wore the crown of all her past,
Two eyes her constant and eternal stars,
Comrade and sovereign eyes that claimed her soul
Lids known through many lives, large frames of love.
He met in her regard his future's gaze,
A promise and a presence and a fire,
Saw an embodiment of aeonic dreams,
A mystery of the rapture for which all
Yearns in this world of brief mortality
Made in material shape his very own.

Savitri: Book V, Canto 2, p. 449

Commentary

The Embodiment of Aeonic Dreams

The gaze of Satyavan and Savitri comes from the glances of the mortal lid. Their faces are lit by the shine of the Supramental Light. Seen of both is the extension of the subtle aura the secret glances of their bodies. Yet in the outer play of love is the inner vision of the Supramental Light. Savitri's psychic gaze comprehends the lids of Satyavan. Open to both are the buried memories of past incarnations which have brought to each the kisses of the past. Satyavan's eyes in a futuristic glance read in the air occult the presence of the spiritual fire of Savitri. In aeonic dreams of the brief human hour, Satyavan nourishes the immaculate delight of a woman's shape.

DETAILED NOTES

355. *Gaze*

The material glance of love filling the lids of Satyavan and Savitri.

356. *An Arc of Meditating Light*

The aura of the subtle body of Satyavan.

357. *Inner Vision*

The Inner vision of Savitri feels the Ray flashing from the forehead of Satyavan.

358. *Many Lives*

The previous incarnations of Satyavan and Savitri.

359. *His Future's Gaze*

In a rare prescience, Satyavan senses futurity and a predestined struggle of Savitri with Yama for his return to the earth.

360. *Aeonic Dreams*

The dreams of the Supermind subtly surging in the body.

361. *Material Shape*

The incarnate life of Savitri symbolised in the woman's form.

58

THE MARRIAGE

He gathered all Savitri into his clasp,
Around her his embrace became the sign
Of a locked closeness through slow intimate years,
A first sweet summary of delight to come
One brevity intense of all long life.
In a wide moment of two souls that meet

She felt her being flow into him as in waves
A river pours into a mighty sea.

Savitri: Book V, Canto 3, p. 464

Commentary

The Material Clasp

The clasp of the lovers is of body and body and their closeness is the closeness of intimate touch. The earthly love is the hints of the immaculate delight of the Absolute Ray.

DETAILED NOTES

362. *A Locked Closeness*

The closeness of matter and matter.

363. *Summary*

Love's delight on earth is the fore-runner of the bliss above. For the Love below and love above are one. Both the physical and the spiritual are the expressions of the One Divine.

364. *Her Being*

The aura of the bodies of the lovers in psychic communion.

59

NARAD TO SAVITRI

He flung on her his vast immortal look;
His inner gaze surrounded her with its light
And reining back knowledge from his immortal lips
He cried to her, who is this that comes, the bride,
The flame-born, and round her illumined head
Pouring their lights, her hymeneal pomps
Move flashing about her ? From what glimmer of glades
Retreating into dewy silences
Or half-seen verge of waters moon-betrayed

Bringst thou this glory of enchanted eyes?
Earth has gold-hued expanses, shadowy hills
That cowl their dreaming phantom heads in night.
And guarded in a cloistral joy of woods,
Screened banks sink down into felicity
Seized by the curved incessant yearning hands
And ripple-passion of the up-gazing stream:
Amid cool-lipped murmurs of its pure embrace
They lose their souls on beds of trembling reeds.
And all these are mysterious presences
In which some spirit's immortal bliss is felt,
And they betray the earth-born heart to joy.
There hast thou paused, and marvelling borne eyes
Unknown, or heard a voice that forced thy life
To strain its rapture through thy listening soul?
Or, if my thought could trust this shimmering gaze,
It would say: thou hast not drunk from an earthly cup,
But stepping through azure curtains of the morn
Thou wast surrounded on a magic verge
In brighter countries than man's eyes can bear."

Savitri: Book VI, Canto 1, p. 475

Commentary

Narad's Perception of Savitri

Casting his shimmering gaze upon Savitri, Narad the sage, in a single glance seizes the sense of the Supramental behind the outer body of Savitri. The bride he knows not as the trick of earth but as the bride of heaven. Narad's sight is a well-head of the rare perception. Around her hair he sees the play of the rays of the Supermind. Before him fall all the delusions of the material sight. For he sees behind the veils of Savitri's body the unveiled delight of the Absolute.

DETAILED NOTES

365. *Immortal Look*

The Supramental gaze which sees through all the veils of matter.

366. *Illumined Head*
The auric light of Supermind circling the forehead of Savitri.

367. *Glory of Enchanted Eyes*
The radiance of the Supramental Light in the eyes of Savitri.

368. *This Shimmering Gaze*
The cosmic gaze of Narad.

369. *Stepping Through Azure Curtains of the Morn*
The descent of Savitri from the planes of the Supermind.

370. *Brighter Countries*
The worlds of the Supramental Light too bright to hear for mortal eyes but for Savitri her native home.

60

SAVITRI'S BODY

Her body like a brimmed pitcher of delight shaped in a splendour of goldcoloured bronze as if to seize earth's truth of hidden bliss. Dream-made illumined mirrors are her eyes.

Draped subtly in a slumberous fringe of jet,
Retaining heaven's reflections in their depths.
Even as her body, such is she within,
Heaven's lustrous morning gloriously recur,
Like drops of fire upon a silver page,
In her young spirit yet untouched with tears.
All beautiful things eternal seem and new
To virgin wonder in her crystal soul

Savitri: Book VI, Canto 1, p. 479

Commentary

The Form of Savitri

Savitri's body is as a pitcher of the Light that spills in over—

running measure the radiances of the hidden Bliss. In her eyes are mirrored the lustrous beams of the Supermind. Within the drapery of her body drops the quenchless fire of the Absolute Ray. The star of youth shines in her eyes; a Virgin wonder crowns her soul.

DETAILED NOTES

371. *Her Body*

Savitri's body is not the body of the surface seeing. It is the material manifestation of the Supramental Radiance.

372. *Within*

The psychic being within the outer body of Savitri.

373. *Pitcher*

The ovoid shape of the body with its aura as seen by the clairvoyant eye.

374. *Drops of Fire*

The shine of aureate delight of Supermind in Savitri's subtle body.

375. *Virgin Wonder*

The ever-renovate eternity of the Supramental Light in the body of Savitri.

61

SAVITRI'S FUTURE

As grows the great and golden bounteous tree
Flowering by Alakananda's murmuring waves,
Where with enamoured speed the waters run
Lisping and babbling to the splendour of morn
And cling with lyric laughter round the knees
Of heaven's daughters dripping magic rain
Pearl-bright from moon-gold limbs and cloudy hair,
So are her dawns like jewelled leaves of light.
So casts she her felicity on men.

A flame of radiant happiness she was born,
And surely will that flame set earth alight.

Savitri: Book VI, Canto 1, pp. 479-480

Commentary

The Flame of Savitri

The flame within the mortal form of Savitri possesses all the potencies of the Supramental Fire to illumine the darkened spaces of the material domain. Savitri is the symbol of the dawn which scatters the shadows of the dark and then in the power of the noonday light destroys the Night of Nescience. From growth to growth the Supramental illumination within her transmutes the darkness of earth into the Radiance Divine.

DETAILED NOTES

376. *Bounteous Tree*

As a tree from the first shoot blossoms into leaf and bloom, so the light of Savitri evolves from Matter and Life into Supermind.

377. *Felicity*

The Supramental Bliss shed in a flourish of power upon the hearts of men.

378. *Flame*

The concealed Light of the Supermind beneath the show of matter set to illumine all the fields of matter.

379. *Earth Alight*

The earth lit by the Light of Savitri.

62

PROPHECY OF THE DEATH OF SATYAVAN

Narad predicts Satyavan's future.

In one brief year when this bright hour flies back
And perches careless on a branch of Time,

This sovereign glory ends heaven lent to earth,
This splendour vanishes from the mortal's sky:
Heaven's greatness came, but was too great to stay.
Twelve swift-winged months are given to him and her;
This day returning Satyavan must die.

Savitri: Book VI, Canto 1, p. 489

Commentary

The Fated Hour

Narad's prediction of the doom of Satyavan and Savitri looms imminent above the wedded pair. Death—that grim jest of infinity—mars with menaces the brief span of their married bliss. The embodied ray of Savitri is a radiance too great to stay. At the appointed moment Yama separates Savitri from Satyavan.

DETAILED NOTES

380. *Brief Year*

The twelve months of married bliss predicted by Narad.

63

THE WORLD DESTINY OF SAVITRI

As a star, uncompanioned, moves in heaven
Unastonished by the immensities of space,
Travelling infinity by its own light,
The great are strongest when they stand alone.
A God-given might of being is their force,
A ray from self's solitude of light the guide;
The soul that can live alone with itself meets God;
Its lonely universe is their rendezvous.
A day may come when she must stand unhelped
On a dangerous brink of the world's doom and hers,
Carrying the world's future on her lonely breast,
Carrying the human hope in a heart left sole
To conquer or fall on a last desperate verge.

Alone with death and close to extinction's edge,
Her single greatness in that last dire scene,
She must cross alone a perilous bridge in Time
And reach an apex of world-destiny
Where all is won or all is lost for man.

Savitri: Book VI, Canto 2, pp. 521-522

Commentary

An Apex of World Destiny

Savitri is helped by no mortal hand. Her soul is a lonely ray in the solitude of God's bliss. On the dangerous brink of the world doom the carrier of the Ray, close to extinction's verge upon the bridge of Time, Savitri stands at the last pinnacle of world destiny to conquer or to die, in answer to the challenge of death.

DETAILED NOTES

381. *A Star*

The Supramental Beam is one light. It moves as a long Ray in Savitri's soul for the world's transformation.

382. *Alone*

The single light of Supermind is Savitri's sole support.

383. *A Ray*

The single light of Supermind.

384. *Dangerous Brink of the world's Doom*

The crisis of Matter at the point of transmutation into Supermind.

385. *Carrying the World's Future*

Savitri is the symbol of the Cosmic Force, bearing in her hands the promise of the change of Body, Mind and Life into Supermind.

386. *Close to Extinction's Edge*

The edge of the crisis when the world of Body, Mind and Life is to change into the Supramental Light.

387. *Bridge in Time*

Nought but the Supramental Light can cross the bridge linking the body of temporal matter with the Supermind.

388. *Apex of World Destiny*

The summit of the destiny of Savitri in her work to change all matter in Light.

389. *Where All is One*

The victory of the Supramental Light over the Asura of Death.

390. *All is Lost for Man*

The challenge of the God of Death to destroy the material worlds of the Supramental Light.

64
BLACK INFINITY

A formless Dread with shapeless endless wings
Filling the universe with its dangerous breath,
A denser darkness than the Night could bear,
Enveloped the heavens and possessed the earth.
A rolling surge of silent death, it came
Curving round the far edge of the quaking globe;
Effacing heaven with its enormous stride
It willed to expunge the choked and anguished air
And end the fable of the joy of life.
It seemed her very being to forbid,
Abolishing all by which her nature lived,
and laboured to blot out her body and soul,
A clutch of some half-seen Invisible,
An ocean of terror and of sovereign might,
A person and a black infinity.

Savitri: Book VII, Canto 6, pp. 606-607

Commentary

The Black Infinity

There appears to Savitri the formless dread Black Infinity—death's terror shrouding the heavens, possessing the earth, effacing the skies, expunging the joy of life, labouring to blot out body and soul. It is this asura of death, the spoiler of light, which the Supramental Light has willed to destroy.

DETAILED NOTES

391. *A Formless Dread*

The figure of Yama which the Light of Savitri meets to slay.

392. *Enveloped*

Death's vast dominion over all the world's of Matter.

393. *Effacing*

The Asuric force which seeks to extinguish all the Lights of heaven.

394. *A Black Infinity*

Death.

65

SAVITRI'S PRAYER

In the hush of the profound and intimate night
She turned to the face of a veiled voiceless Truth
Hid in the dumb recesses of the heart
Or waiting beyond the last peak climbed by Thought,—
Unseen itself it sees the struggling world
And prompts our quest, but cares not to be found,—
Out of that distant vast came a reply.
Something unknown, unreached, inscrutable
Sent down the messages of its bodiless Light,
Cast lightning flashes of a thought not ours

Crossing the immobile silence of her mind:
In its might of irresponsible sovereignty
It seized on speech to give those flamings shape,
Made beat the heart of wisdom in a word
and spoke immortal things through mortal lips.
Savitri: Book VII, Canto 7, p. 627

Commentary

The Invocation to the Supramental Light

In the profound hush of her being, sensing the slow and certain steps of Yama's approach to seize with ruthless grasp the life of Satyavan, Savitri invokes the power of the Supramental Ray which resides in the apparent dumbness of the silence of her heart to descend to destroy the dark designs of Death. In answer to her prayer from the immobile silences of her mind, the flaming shape of the Absolute Radiance through the mortal lips of Savitri gives the assurance of the destruction of the form of terror—Death.

DETAILED NOTES

395. *Voiceless Truth*

The supramental truths of Supermind concealed in the dress of matter.

396. *Dumb Recesses*

The Supermind in the depths of matter.

397. *The Last Peak*

The last ranges of the Supramental light.

398. *Something Unknown*

The concealed Supramental Light.

399. *Bodiless Light*

The Ray of the Supermind in absolute sovereignty.

66

SAVITRI'S CHANGED CONSCIOUSNESS

She was Space and the wideness of his days.
From this she rose where Time and Space were not;
The superconscient was her native air,
Infinity was her movements' natural space;
Eternity looked out from her own Time.

Savitri: Book VII, Canto 7, p. 632

Commentary

Savitri's Transmutation

In the silence and the hush Savitri drops for Satyavan her vesture and her form revealing herself as the Infinite Consciousness bending over the sides of Satyavan's ending days. She shows herself to Satyavan as the Spaceless and the Timeless. From regions of the superconscient air, out of matter's depth, emerge the revealed eternities of Savitri ready for the battle with the God of Death.

DETAILED NOTES

400. *Native Air*

The native air of the Supermind behind embodied Savitri.

401. *Infinity*

The natural infinity of the Supramental Light in an enamoured poise above the brows of Satyavan.

402. *Eternity*

The Timeless Sovereign, the Absolute Light.

67

THE DEATH OF SATYAVAN

But now his sweet familiar hue was changed
Into a tarnished greyness and his eyes

Dimmed over, forsaken of the clear light she loved.
Only the dull and physical mind was left,
Vacant of the bright spirit's luminous gaze.
But once before it faded wholly back,
He cried out in a clinging last despair,
"Savitri, Savitri, O Savitri,
Lean down, my soul, and kiss me while I die."
And even as her pallid lips pressed his,
His failed, losing last sweetness of response;
His cheeks pressed down her golden arm. She sought
His mouth still with her living mouth, as if
She could persuade his soul back with her kiss;
Then grew aware they were no more alone.

Savitri: Book VIII, Canto 3, p. 639

Commentary

The Separating Hand of Death

The remorseless power of Death in persistent pursuit seeks the life of Satyavan. Satyavan in the arms of Savitri sinks into slumber, struck by the cold touch of Yama. Satyavan's dim eyes with a last shine sighs for the lips of Savitri. In the greyness of the material plane vain is her kiss. In their physical severance Savitri and Satyavan find the presence of the veiled Asura—Death.

DETAILED NOTES

403. *Dimmed*

In the receding of the spirit of Satyavan matter loses its materiality to the soul. It appears as the shadow of material things.

404. *Losing*

In the material dissolving of the body of Satyavan all response of matter is lost. The body's death is the spirit's liberation.

405. *No More Alone*

In the passing of Satyavan the wedded pair is not alone. Between the pair is the shadow of Death which the light of Savitri is destined to destroy.

68

SAVITRI'S DEFIANCE OF DEATH

"I bow not to thee, O huge mask of Death,
Black lie of night the cowed soul of man,
Unreal, inescapable end of things,
Thou grim jest played with the immortal spirit.
Conscious of immortality I walk.
A victor spirit conscious of my force,
Not as a suppliant to thy gates I came:
Unslain I have survived the clutch of Night.
My first strong grief moves not my seated mind;
My unwept tears have turned to pearls of strength:
I have transformed my ill-shaped brittle clay
Into the hardness of a statued soul.
Now in the wrestling of the splendid gods
My spirit shall be obstinate and strong
Against the vast refusals of the world.
I stoop not with the subject mob of minds
Who run to glean with eager satisfied hands
And pick from its mire mid many trampling feet
Its scornful small consciousness to the weak.
Mine is the labour of the battling gods:
Imposing on the slow reluctant years
The flaming will that reigns beyond the stars,
They lay the law of Mind on Matter's works
And win the soul's wish from earth's inconscient force.

Savitri: Book IX, Canto 2, p. 664

Commentary

The Wrestle with Yama, the God of Death

The spirit of Savitri armed with the sword of the Supramental Ray, defiant and determined, proceeds to slay the dragon, Death. The immortal light within her knows the grim jest played by the Light Divine, knows the truth behind the lie of the nought, the radiance behind the cowl of Yama. Out of the tears of time, transformed from the bonds of matter into the sculptured shape of soul, refusing to accede to the harsh accents of Yama, battling with the forces of the Asuric night, her flaming will impose upon matter the reign of the Supramental Ray in its conquering victory over the forces of the inconscient.

DETAILED NOTES

406. *Mask of Death*

The mask of Death is but a veil o the Supramental Light.

407. *Life of Night*

The falsehood of the world of Matter, Mind and Life.

408. *Grim Jest*

The jest of Death played upon the immortal soul.

409. *Grief*

Grief born of the world of matter is a falsehood which the immortal spirit within Savitri will not accept.

410. *Transformed*

The transformation of the Body, Mind and Life of Savitri back into Supramental substance.

411. *Wrestling*

The battle of the Ray with the God of Death.

412. *Imposing*

The imposition of the reign of Light upon the world of Matter, Mind and Life.

69

THE DEMAND FOR SATYAVAN

But Savitri answered the disdainful Shade:
"World-spirit, I was thy equal spirit born.
I am immortal in my mortality.

I tremble not before the immobile gaze
Of the unchanging marble hierarchies
That look with the stone eyes of Law and Fate.
My soul can meet them with its living fire.
Out of thy shadow give me back again
Into earth's flowering spaces Satyavan
In the sweet transiency of human limbs
To do with him my spirit's burning will.

Savitri: Book IX, Canto 2, pp. 665-666

Commentary

Savitri's Answer to the Shade

The soul of Savitri throws down the gauntlet of defiance before the Death. Her soul in equal sovereignty with the soul of Yama demands for herself no heaven of transcendence in the life of the ascending spheres. The Transciency of earthly limbs is the seeking of her radiant eyes. The Supramental vision of Savitri is aware of the Light in matter's inconscient sheath. From Yama she extracts the promise of Satyavan's return to earth.

DETAILED NOTES

413. *Shade*

The shade of Death concealing the Face of the Supermind.

414. *World's Spirit*

The cosmic form of Death in the veiled depth of matter.

415. *Marble Hierarchies*

The Karmic laws of life which carry the stony will of the darkening law in matter's crypt.

416. *Give Me Back*

The restoration of Satyavan in matter transmuted into Supermind.

417. *My Spirit's Burning Will*

Savitri's will to transform body, mind and life into the Supermind.

70

SAVITRI'S TRIUMPH OVER DEATH

My heart is stronger than thy bonds, O Death.
It sees and feels the one Heart beat in all,
It feels the high Transcendent's sunlike hands,
It sees the cosmic Spirit at its work:
In the dim Night it lies alone with God.
My heart's strength can carry the grief of the universe
And never falter from its luminous track,
Its white tremendous orbit through God's peace.
It can drink up the sea of All-Delight
And never lose the white spiritual touch,
The calm that broods in the deep Infinite.

Savitri : Book X, Canto 3, pp. 713-714

Commentary

The White Spiritual Touch of Savitri

The white spiritual touch of Savitri on the luminous track of the Supramental manifestation breaks the veils of Death. With hands transcendent she shakes the soul of Yama. She carries the griefs of our universe and shatters the brittle vase of tears. Her cosmic spirit liberates the Light in the dumb recesses of matter.

DETAILED NOTES

418. *Bonds*

The falsity of the body of matter, Death.

419. *Luminous Track*

The paths of the Supramental manifestation.

420. *The White Spiritual Touch*

The touch of the Supramental Light upon the flesh.

71

THE ASCENT TO THE PEAKS

A few have dared the last supreme ascent
And break through borders of blinding light above,
And feel a breath around of mightier air,
Receive a vaster being's messages
And baths in its immense intuitive Ray.
On summit Mind are radiant altitudes
Exposed to the lustre of Infinity,
Outskirts and dependencies of the house of Truth,
Upraised estates of Mind and measureless.
There man can visit but there he cannot live.
A cosmic thought spreads out its vastitudes;
Its smallest parts are here philosophies
Challenging with their detailed immensity,
Each figuring an omniscient scheme of things.
But higher still can climb the ascending light;
There are vasts of vision and eternal suns,
Oceans of an immortal luminousness,
Flame-hills assaulting heaven with their peaks,
There dwelling all becomes a blaze of sight;
A burning head of vision leads the mind,
Thought trails behind it its long comet tail;
The heart glows, an illuminate and seer,
And sense is kindled into identity.
A highest flight climbs to a deepest view:
In a wide opening of its native sky
Intuition's lightnings range in a bright pack
Hunting all hidden truths out of their lairs,
Its fiery edge of seeing absolute
Cleaves into locked unknown retreats of self,
Rummages the sky-recesses of the brain,
Lights up the occult chambers of the heart.

Savitri : Book X, Canto 4, p. 740

Commentary

The Unknown Retreats of the Light

The daring spirit of Savitri scales the peak of the Supreme ascent. Breaking through the borders of the Intuitive Ray, passing beyond the outskirts and dependencies of Truth Savitri arrives in the bright halls of the Supermind. Beyond Supermind Savitri sees the flame hills of the Triune Ecstasies. There all being becomes a blaze of sight. There thought is transformed into conscious existence, heart into conscious bliss and sense into supramental vision in identity with the Cosmic Whole. There intuitions lightening opens the hidden layers of truth. There are unsealed the unseen retreats of the Absolute Self. There in the occult chambers of the Light all is clear and luminous.

DETAILED NOTES

421. *Supreme Ascent*

The realms of the Triune Ecstasies.

422. *Intuitive Ray*

The regions of the Intuitive Light.

423. *Outskirts and Dependencies*

The seven fields of the rare substances springing from the creative action of the Supermind.

424. *Omniscient Scene*

The whole cosmic order of worlds rare and gross created by the Supermind.

425. *Blaze of Sight*

The dazzling fields of Supermind.

426. *Identity*

The final union of the soul in the field of the Triune Ecstasies.

427. *Intuition's Lightning*

The flash of the Intuitive Ranges.

428. *Unknown Retreats*

The hidden fields of the substances rare or gross of the Self.

429. *Lights*

The Supramental illumination within the occult heart of man.

72

SUPERMIND

Savitri through Integral Yoga attained the transformed consciousness of the Supermind

There is a world of everlasting Light,
In the realms of the immortal Supermind
Truth who hides here her head in mystery,
Her riddle deemed by reason impossible
In the stark structure of material form,
Unenigmaed lives, unmasked her face and there
Is Nature and the common law of things.
There in a body made of spirit stuff,
The hearth-stone of the everlasting Fire,
Action translates the movements of the soul,
Thought steps infallible and absolute
And life is continual worship's rite,
A sacrifice of rapture to the One.
A cosmic vision, a spiritual sense
Feels all the Infinite lodged in finite form
And seen through a quivering ecstasy of light
Discovers the bright face of the Bodiless.

Savitri : Book X, Canto 4, pp. 742-743

Commentary

The Bright Face of the Bodiless

Rolling through ascending worlds, beyond the ranges of Mind, Higher Mind and Over-mind the spirit of Savitri in trance returns to her native air the realm of the Supermind. There are unmasked all the falsehood of Body, Mind and Life. There all substance is woven of the Spirit's stuff. There all life is the worship of the One. There the bounded finite becomes the unbounded Infinite. There the Bodiless reveals the bright face of the Absolute Ray.

DETAILED NOTES

430. *Supermind*

The region of the creative Ray.

431. *Unmasked*

The unveiling of the Supramental light in all matter.

432. *A Body*

The body of the Supramental Light.

433. *The One*

The Absolute Ray.

434. *Finite Form*

The bounded form of the Infinite and the physical veil of the Supramental Light.

435. *Face of the Bodiless*

The embodied form of the Absolute Light.

73

THE ABYSS OF SAPPHIRE

Savitri also reached the subtle planes of the universal Self in the Abyss of Sapphire.

In serene arches of translucant calm
From Wonder's dream-vasts cloudless skies slid down
An abyss of sapphire; sunlight visited eyes
Which suffered without pain the absolute ray
And saw immortal clarities of form.

Twilight and mist were exiles from that air,
Night was impossible to such radient heavens.
Firm in the bosom of immensity
Spiritual breadths were seen, sublimely born
From a still beauty of creative joy;
Embodied thoughts to sweet dimensions held
To please some carelessness of divine peace,
Answered the deep demand of an infinite sense
And its need of forms to house its bodiless thrill.
A march of universal power in Time,
The harmonic order of self's vastitudes
In cyclic symmetries and metric planes
Harboured a cosmic rapture's revelry
In an endless figuring of the spirit in things
Planned by the artist who has dreamed the worlds.

Savitri: Book XI, Canto 1, pp. 753-754

Commentary

The Harmonic Order of the Divine Vastitudes

In her swift ascent to the Supermind the plural vastitudes of the life of God open in cosmic clarities to the radiant eyes of Savitri. The cloudless skies of the Supramental Ray descend without hurt into the orbs of her infinite seeing. For her are the radiant morns of the Supramental day. Twilight and mist are absent from her native air. Darkness there has no place. There the Infinite Delight needing an infinite form thrills in Infinite space. Plane within plane of matter rare reveal the rapture of the plan which the Architect of Eternity builds in the secret substances of God.

DETAILED NOTES

436. *Cloudless Skies*

The cloudless skies of the Supermind.

437. *An Abyss of Sapphire*

The crystal sphere of the Supermind.

438. *Immortal Clarities*

The Divine clarities free of the illusion.

439. *Twilight*

The symbol of the mists of lower matter.

440. *Night*

In the Supermind there is no Asuric night.

441. *Need of Form*

The subtle form of the infinite Light in the regions of the Supermind.

442. *Self's Vastitudes*

Range above range of the subtle fields of God.

443. *Planned*

The cosmic design to create for man the fields of the Absolute Delight.

74

THE PILGRIM MULTITUDE

Savitri saw the pilgrim multitude, the human race transformed entering the planes of the Supermind.

Eternal mountains ridge on gleaming ridge
Whose lines were graved as on a sapphire plate
And etched the borders of heaven's lustrous noon
Climbed like piled temple stairs and from their heads
Of topless meditation heard below
The approach of a blue pilgrim multitude
And listened to a great arriving voice
Of the wide travel hymn of timeless seas.
A chanting crowd from mountain bosom slipped
Past branches fragrant with a sigh of flowers
Hurrying through sweetnesses with revel leaps;
The murmurous rivers of felicity
Divinely rippled, honey-voiced desires,

Mingling their sister eddies of delight,
Then, widening to a pace of calm-lipped muse
Down many-blimmered estuaries of dream
Went whispering into lakes of liquid peace.
On a brink held of senseless ecstasy
And guarding an eternal poise of thought
Sat sculptured souls dreaming by rivers of sound
In changeless attitudes of marble bliss.
Around her lived the children of God's day
In an unspeakable felicity,
A happiness never lost, the immortal's ease,
A glad eternity's blissful multitude.
Around, the deathless nations moved and spoke,
Souls of a luminous celestial joy,
Faces of stark beauty, limbs of the moulded Ray;
In cities out like gems of conscious stone
And wonderful pastures and on gleaming coasts
Bright forms were seem, eternity's luminous tribes
Above her rhythming godheads whirled the spheres,
Rapt mobile fixities here blindly sought
By the huge erring orbits of our stars.
Ecstatic voices smote at hearing's chords,
Each movement found a music all its own;
Songs thrilled of birds upon unfading boughs,
The colours of whose plumage had been caught
From the rainbow of imagination's wings.
Immortal fragrance packed the quivering breeze,
In groves that seemed moved bosoms and trembling depths
The million children of the undying spring
Bloomed, pure unnumbered stars of hued delight
Nestling for shelter in their emerald sky.

Savitri : Book XI, Canto 1, pp. 755-756

Commentary

Souls in the City of the White Beatitudes

The gleaming ridges of the Supermind break upon the lids of Savitri. The children of the Sun crowd upon crowd, hurry to the city of God. In the Eden of the rare delight murmuring rivulets race through the meads of joy. Passing the eddies of wondrous streams, traversing the many glimmered estuaries of undreamt delight, the bright eyes of Savitri behold in marble bliss the Masters of the Light. There the un-sumbered children of the day with bodies of moulded calm arrive at the gemmed cities of the Light. Bright are the forms of the luminous tribes of God where the whirling spheres, ecstatic voices and birds of varied plunage, chant their song unheard of the human ear. In the pavilions of delight is the shelter of the blue pilgrims of the unfading Ray.

DETAILED NOTES

444. *Ridge*

The ranges of the Supermind.

445. *Blue Pilgrims*

The votaries of the Supermind.

446. *Eddies of Delight*

The eddies of the streams in the fields of delight.

447. *Sculptured Souls*

The Adepts of the Ray.

448. *Cities*

The cities of the Light.

449. *The Spheres*

The spheres of the seven ascending substances whirling around the worlds of the Supermind.

450. *Emerald Sky*

The subtle hues of the Heaven of the Supermind.

75

THE CROWN OF SAVITRI'S ASCENT

Savitri saw nobler worlds where the finite and the Infinite blend.

These were but sumptuous decorated doors
To worlds nobler, more felicitously fair.

Endless aspired the climbing of those heavens;
Realm upon realm received her soaring view.
Then on what seemed one crown of the ascent
Where finite and the infinite are one,
Immune she beheld the strong immortal's seats
Who live for a celestial joy and rule
The middle regions of the unfading Ray.
Great forms of deities sat in deathless tiers,
Eyes of an unborn gaze towards her leaned
Through a transparency of crystal fire
In the beauty of bodies wrought from rapture's lines,
Shapes of entrancing sweetness stilling bliss,
Feet glimmering upon the sun-stone courts of mind,
Heaven's cup-bearers bore round the Eternal's wine;
A tangle of bright bodies, of moved souls
Tracing the close and intertwined delight,
The harmonious tread of lives for ever joined
In the passionate oneness of a mystic joy
As if sun-beams made living and divine,
The golden-bosomed Apsara goddesses,
In groves flooded from an argent disk of bliss
That floated through a luminous sapphire dream,
In a cloud of raiment lit with golden limbs
And gleaming footfalls treading faery swards,
Virgin motions of bacchant innocences
Who know their riot for a dance of God.
Whirled linked in moonlit revels of the heart.
Impeccable artists of unerring forms,
Magician builders of sound and rhythmic words,
Wind-haired Gandharvas chanted to the ear
The odes that shape the universal thought,
The lines that tear the veil from Deity's face,
The rhythms that bring the sounds of wisdom's sea.

Savitri: Book XI, Canto 1, pp. 759-760.

Commentary

The Unveiling of the Divinity

From the decorated doors of the ascensions of the seven worlds of the rare substances, from the middle regions of the undying ray, from the mind of Light into the fields of the Overmind, the spirit of Savitri explores the terrain of the countries of the Supermind. On the crown of the ascent of the Supermind, on the summit and head of creative life, the Supramental illumination unveils the subtlest sights and scenes of the Absolute Ray.

DETAILED NOTES

451. *Decorated Doors*

The door from door to the worlds of the rare substances.

452. *Crown of the Ascent of Supermind*

Where the finite and infinite blend.

453. *Middle Regions*

The middle regions of the Overmind leading to the ranges of the Supermind.

454. *A Tangle of Bright Bodies*

The group-souls of the group-life of the higher heavenly spheres where individual spirits blend with other spirits.

455. *Ever-Joined*

The group-souls intertwined and blended.

456. *Argent Disc of Bliss*

The bright sphere of the bliss.

457. *Dance of God*

The whirl of atoms of matter rare or gross of the ascending fields of substance.

458. *Magicial Builders*

The masters of form.

459. *The Veil*

The veil of God which discloses the Divine behind all phenomena.

76

DEATH'S TRANSFIGURATION

In the final ascent of Savitri into Supermind, Death, the pitiless snarer, the mask of God, was transfigured into the wondrous face of the Supreme.

As one drowned in a sea of splendour and bliss
Mute in the maze of these surprising worlds
Turning she saw their living knot and source,
Key to their charm and fount of their delight,
And knew him for the same who snares our lives
Captured in his terrifying pitiless met,
And makes the universe his prison camp
And makes in his immense and vacant vasts
The labour of the stars a circuit vain
And death the end of every human road
And grief and pain the wages of man's toil.
One whom her soul had faced as Death and Night
A sum of all sweetness gathered into his limbs
And blinded her heart to the beauty of the suns.
Transfigured was the formidable shape.
His darkness and his sad destroying might
Abolishing for ever and disclosing
The mystery of his high and violent deeds,
A secret splendour rose revealed to sight
Where once the vast embodied Void had stood.
Night the dim mask had grown a wonderful face.
The vague infinity was slain whose gloom
Had outlined from the terrible Unknown
The obscure disastrous figure of a god,
Fled was the error that arms the hands of grief,
And lighted the ignorant gulf whose hollow deeps
Had given to nothingness a dreadful voice.
As when before the eye that wakes in sleep
Is opened the sombre binding of a book,
Illumined letterings are seen which kept
A golden blaze of thought inscribed within,
A marvellous form responded to her gaze
Whose sweetness justified life's blindest pain;

All Nature's struggle was its easy price,
The universe and its agony seemed worthwhile.
As if the choric calyx of a flower
Aerial, visible on music's waves,
A lotus of light-petalled ecstasy
Took shape out of the tremulous heart of things.
There was no more the torment under the stars,
The evil sheltered behind Nature's mask;
There was no more the dark pretence of hate,
The cruel ictus on Love's altered face.

Savitri: Book XI, Canto 1, pp. 761-762

Commentary

The Reversal of the Face of Yama

In the subtle essence of the Supermind, in the unitarian consciousness into which all creation retires, Savitri beholds in transformed light the secrets of the dark abyss. There the knot of Matter, Mind and Life is unloosed. The face of Yama is unmasked. The veiled God of Death unveils his webs of concealment. In a dramatic reversal Yama is transmuted into the God of Love and Bliss. The snares of Death are the embrace of the Light. Transfigured is the formidable shape of Death. Discovered is the mystery of his violent deeds. In the vasts of the void grows a wondrous face. Slain is all grief; dispersed is all gloom. In the glimmering fields of the Supermind the eye of Savitri awakes to truth; the revelations of that marvellous form justify earth's blindest pain. As a seed dimmed in the dark, dank depths of the soil waxes into the flower, as the white petals of the lotus open to the Sun, so the light of Supermind bared to Savitri the revelations of the Supreme Truth wherein dissolved the falsehood of Death.

DETAILED NOTES

460. *Living Knot*

The Knot of Matter, Mind and Life.

461. *Source*

The creative field of Supermind.

462. The net of the mental illusions which hides the face of God behind the mask of Yama.

463. *Transfigured*

The transmutation of body, mind and life into Supermind where-in the deceptions of falsehood are dissolved.

464. *Mystery*

The mystery of Yama discovered to be the mystery of the Supramental Light in the play of the mask of Death.

465. *A Wonderful Face*

The face of God behind the mask of Yama.

466. *The Eye that Wakes*

The Supramental vision which wakes Night's slumber.

467. *A Marvellous Form*

The form of God behind the mask of Death.

468. *Justified*

The divine justification of the fall of the soul into the worlds of suffering.

469. *Pretence of Fate*

The play of Love behind the mask of Death.

470. *Loves Altered Face*

The play of the Divine behind the veil involves two reversals. First, the Force of Love is changed into the Force of Death. Second, the Force of Death is changed into the Force of Love.

77

THE INVIOLABLE ECSTASY

The Supreme Ecstasy, the Absolute
Ray spoke to Savitri of her mission.

I am the hushed search of the jealous gods
Pursuing my wisdom's vast mysterious work

Seized in the thousand meeting ways of heaven.
I am the beauty of the unveiled Ray
Drawing through the deep roads of the infinite might
The unconquerable pilgrim soul of earth
Beneath the flaring torches of the stars.
I am the inviolable Ecstasy;
They who have looked on me, shall grieve no more.
The eyes that live in night shall see my form.

Savitri : Book XI, Canto 1, p. 767

Commentary

The Unveiling of the Ray

In subtle speech which is to human ears a silence, the Absolute Ray unveils the mysteries of its walk in the worlds of matter. It drops all the masks of grossness. It shows itself as the Divine Face of the Ecstasies and gives to the broken heart of Savitri the messages of the Light. It assures her that no grief for Satyavan will mar her mind. For her eyes will see the Light behind the mists of Form.

DETAILED NOTES

471. *Hushed Search*

The search for the Supramental Ray in the heart of matter.

472. *Mysterious Work*

The occult operations of the Supermind in the world of matter.

473. *Unveiled Ray*

The uncreated Ray of the Absolute free of the veils of Matter, Mind and Life.

474. *The Inviolable Ecstasy*

The bliss of the Absolute Ray.

78

INVITATION TO TRANSCENDENCE

The Absolute Spirit invited Savitri to dwell in the Bliss of transcendence leaving Satyavan and the earth.

Above the wash and surge of Time and Space,
Disengaging from the cosmic commonalty
By which all life is kin in and joy,
Delivered from the universal Law
The sun-like single and transcendent spirit
Can blaze its way through the minds' barrier wall
And burn alone in the eternal sky,
Inhabitant of a wide and endless calm.
O flame, withdraw into thy luminous self
Or else return to thy original might
On a seer-summit above thought and world.

Savitri : Book XI, Canto 1, pp. 775-776

Commentary

The Temptation of Savitri

The unveiled Divine even after the falling of the mask of Death puts the Soul of Savitri to the test of the aspiration. It transmits to her soul a choice a retreat into the worlds of the luminous self, a lodging in the ranges of the Supermind, a total abandonment, of the fields of the earth, a transcendence of matter, mind and life or a return to the field of Death and desire.

DETAILED NOTES

475. *Burn Alone*

The individual soul dwelling alone in the solitude of God.

476. *O Flame*

The light within the body of Savitri.

477. *Withdraw*

The withdrawal into Supermind.

478. *Seer Summit*

The summit of the Mind of Light and Overmind.

79

THE ETERNAL THOUGHT

Savitri heard the voice of Eternal Thought prompting her to seize the Perfect Bliss of Nirvana.

Upon the falling sound
A power went forth that shook the founded spheres
And loosed the stakes that hold the tents of form.
Absolved from vision's grip and the folds of thought,
Rapt from her sense like disappearing scenes
In the stupendous theatre of Space
The heaven-worlds vanished in spiritual light.
A movement was abroad, a cry, a word,
Beginningless in its vast discovery,
Momentless in its unthinkable return;
Choired in calm seas she heard the eternal Thought.
Rhythming itself abroad unutterably
In spaceless orbits and on timeless roads.

Savitri : Book XI, Canto I, p. 780

Commentary

The Voice of the Force

Then the Supramental Force shaking all the tents of form, absolving Savitri from the grip of its vision, vanishing from the tremendous theatre of space, once more whispers into Savitri's ear the prompting of the word to leave the world of gross matter for the world of the white Beatitudes.

DETAILED NOTES

479. *Power*

The Supramental Force.

480. *Tents of Form*

The forms of the subtle worlds.

481. *Absolved from Vision's Grip*

The descending trance of Savitri where-in she loses grip of the subtle worlds in the huge amphitheatre of space.

482. *Eternal Thought*

The voice of the Eternal probing the possible desire of Savitri to abide in the Nirmanic Bliss.

80

THE CHOICE

The Absolute Spirit put before Savitri the choice of Nirvana or a return to earth.

Choose, spirit, thy supreme choice not given again;
For now from my highest being looks at thee
The nameless formless peace where all things rest.
In a happy vast sublime cessation know,
An immense extinction in eternity,
A point that disappears in the infinite,
Felicity of the extinguished flame,
Last sinking of a wave in a boundless sea,
End of the trouble of thy wandering thoughts,
Close of the journeying of thy pilgrim soul.

Savitri : Book XI, Canto 1, p. 781

Commentary

The Sublime Cessation

Once more with a subtle smile the Absolute hints of Savitri to accept a formless peace in the total dissolution of body, mind and matter wherein the point of the finite becomes one with the infinite. It asks Savitri to choose the extinction of the earth life and close of her pilgrimage in the rounds of matter.

DETAILED NOTES

483. *Choice*

The choice between the field of earth where Yama reigns and the field of the Supermind where bliss reigns.

484. *Formless Peace*

The formless peace of Nirvana in which all forms of pain are dissolved.

485. *Sublime Cessation*

Cessation of the suffering field of Matter, Mind and Life in the attainment of Nirvana.

486. *Extinction*

Nirvana.

487. *A Point*

The point where the individual life merges into the Infinite.

488. *Close*

The end of physical incarnations.

81

THE PROMISE OF THE INFINITE

Savitri refuses to live in the ecstatic bliss of Nirvana. She chooses earth as her sphere of action. The Infinite gives her assurances of its support.

Now will I do in thee my marvellous works.
I will fasten thy nature with my cords of strength,
Subdue to my delight thy spirit's limbs
And make thee a vivid knot of all my bliss,
And build in thee my proud and crystal home.
Thy days shall be my shafts of power and light,

Thy nights my starry mysteries of joy
And all my clouds lie tangled in thy hair
And all my springtides marry in thy mouth.
O Sun-Wood, thou shalt raise the earth-soul to Light
And bring down God into the lives of men;
Earth shall be my work-chamber and my house,
My garden of life to plant a seed divine.
When all thy work in human time is done,
The mind of earth shall be a home of light,
The life of earth a tree a growing towards heaven
The body of earth a tabernacle of God.

Savitri : Book XI, Canto 1, pp. 784-85

Commentary

The Return of Savitri into Matter for Earth's Transmutation

The Supramental Light gives Savitri a fresh pledge for her aspiration to transform the earth's soul into Light. It pours into the triple knot of her being of body, mind and life the hidden ecstasies of the Ray. Savitri becomes the crystal house of light. The starry beams of the Absolute Ray are tangled in her hair. Her lips are a spring-time of delight. Hers is the task to bring into the movements of matter the influx of the Supramental Light. Earth is the field of her work wherein the mind of matter is to house the Light.

DETAILED NOTES

489. *Fasten*

The earth nature of Savitri is subdued to become the unimpeded vehicle of the Ray.

490. *A Vivid Knot*

The Knot of Savitri's being pulsing with the streams of the Absolute Delight.

491. *Build*

The reconstruction of the whole edifice of the material life into Supramental Radiance.

492. *Crystal Home*

The crystal house of the Supramental Light in the cavern of the human heart.

493. *Bring Down God*

The descent of the Supramental Light into matter.

494. *Work Chamber*

The field of Matter, Mind and Life.

495. *A Seed Divine*

The concealed Supermind in the field of matter.

496. *The Mind of Earth*

The trasmutation of the terrestrial unconsciousness into the light of the Supermind.

82

THE NEW RACE

Savitri sees the future of humanity—the new race of the Supramental Manhood.

Some shall be made the glory's receptacles
And vehicles of the Eternal's luminous power.
These are the high forerunners, the heads of Time,
The great deliverers of earth-bound mind,
The high transfigurers of human clay,
This first-born of a new supernal race.
The incarnate dual power shall open God's door,
Eternal supermind touch earthly Time.
The Superman shall wake in mortal man
And manifest the hidden demi-god
Or grow into the God-Light and God-Force
Revealing the secret deity in the cave.

Savitri : Book XI, Canto 1, p. 792

Commentary

Savitri's Supramentalisation of the Earth

The Absolute lays down the plan for the Supramentalisation of the human race. The first born of the new race will be the children of the Supermind. In them the hidden divinity of the Light will be expressed through the vehicles of the Supramental Light. In them mind will be Supermind, the subtle receptacle of the hidden glories of the Ray revealing the deity in the cave.

DETAILED NOTES

497. *Vehicles*
The souls of man will be the channels of the luminous power.

498. *The First Born*
The first of the race of the Supermind.

499. *Deity in the Cave*
The hidden Supermind in matter's depths.

83

THE AWAKENING OF SATYAVAN

Triumphant over death, Savitri returns to earth awakening the sleeping body of Satyavan.

Then sighing to her touch the soft-winged sleep
Rose hovering from his flower-like lips and flew
Murmurous away. Awake, he found her eyes
Waiting for his, and felt her hands, and saw
The earth his home given back to him once more
And her made his again, his passion's all.

Savitri: Book XII, Epilogue, p. 805.

Commentary

The Restoration of the Body of Satyavan

The dynamic action of the Supramental Force restores the

body of Satyavan. Awakening he sees no hand of Death touching his flesh. Around him is the aroma of Savitri. Her hands he feels as he felt before. Her breath he inhales, her lips he touches. For death's shadow was of illusion's eye.

DETAILED NOTES

500. *Awake*

The return of Satyavan from the trance of Death.

501. *Given Back*

The restoration of the earth by the Supramental touch.

502. *Made His Again*

The true marriage of souls in bodies of bliss.

503. *His Passion's All*

Love made complete by the Ray.

84

THE RETURN TO EARTH

Savitri and Satyavan with linked hands go forward to their work of transforming mankind.

Drawn by white manes upon high-roofed car
In flare of the unsteady torches went
With linked hands Satyavan and Savitri,
Hearing a marriage march and nuptial hymn,
Where waited them the many-voiced human world.
Numberless the stars swam on their shadowy field
Describing in the gloom the ways of light.
Then while they skirted yet the southward verge,
Lost in the halo of her musing brows
Night, splendid with the moon dreaming in heaven
In silver peace, possessed her luminous reign.
She brooded through her stillness on a thought
Deep-guarded by her mystic folds of light,
And in her bosom nursed a greater dawn.

Savitri: Book XII, Epilogue, pp.813-814